Lest we forget...

WHITE HATE CRIMES

Other Books by Alphonso Pinkney

The American Way of Violence
Black Americans
The Committed:
> *White Activists in the Civil Rights Movement*

The Myth of Black Progress
Poverty and Politics in Harlem
> *(With Roger Woock)*

Red Black and Green:
> *Black Nationalism in the United States*

Lest we forget . . .

WHITE HATE CRIMES

HOWARD BEACH

AND OTHER RACIAL ATROCITIES

_____

Alphonso Pinkney

THIRD WORLD PRESS • CHICAGO

LEST WE FORGET: WHITE HATE CRIMES
Howard Beach and Other Racial Atrocities

First Edition
First Printing 1994

ISBN: 0-88378-088-7
Library of Congress #: 93-60826

Manufactured in the United States of America.

Third World Press
P.O. Box 19730
Chicago, IL 60619

Cover art and design by Craig Taylor

In Memoriam

Wajid Abdul-Salaam, *35*

Andel Anthony Amos, *19*

Nicholas A. Bartlett, *27*

Eleanor Bumpers, *66*

Robert Cole, *13*

Antoine Davis, *30*

Michael Griffith, *23*

Yusuf Hawkins, *16*

Henry Hughes, *25*

Terence Keane, *29*

Jose Luis Lebron, *14*

Louis Liranso, *17*

Richard Luke, *25*

Mary Mitchell, *41*

Federico Pereira, *21*

Juan Rodriguez, *40*

Luis Rodriguez, *19*

Alfred Sanders, *39*

Yvonne Smallwood, *28*

Samuel B. Spencer III, *20*

Michael Stewart, *25*

Kevin Thorpe, *31*

William Turks, *34*

Derrick Antonio Tyrus, *17*

ACKNOWLEDGEMENTS

I wish to thank several persons for supporting this project: Barbara Lewis, for suggesting the book's title; Donna Williams, my editor at Third World Press; and the staff of the Jefferson Market Branch of the New York Public Library.

CONTENTS

PREFACE

The ascendancy of conservatism inspired by Ronald Reagan's Presidency has brought about drastic changes in American life, not the least of which has been the resurgence of prejudice and violence against minorities. Many civil rights gains made during the last half of the 1960s and during the 1970s were reversed during Reagan's terms in the 1980s.

High-level officials set the ethos for attitudes and behaviors of the masses of United States citizens. While a few were sympathetic to the aspirations of minorities, many more sought to contain or even reverse whatever gains had been made. More than any other high official in the 20th century, President Ronald Reagan created a climate of opinion hostile to the civil rights of minorities. American character being what it is, it did not take long for citizens to translate the Reagan backlash into anti-minority behavior. It was as if white Americans had been anxiously awaiting a leader to confirm their long-standing prejudices. And just as Ronald Reagan was responsible for creating a national climate of hate and violence throughout the

PREFACE

United States, Edward Koch, the former mayor of New York City, championed such behavior in New York City. Koch's litany of anti-Black statements and actions is unparalleled in the recent history of the city.

Throughout American history, minorities, especially people of color, have struggled to force U.S. society to live up to its stated ideals. In some cases they were supported by administrations in Washington, while in others their struggles met strong resistance. The latter was the dominant pattern of the 1980s. While the President was proclaiming his support for minority rights, his behavior was defying his professed attitudes.

It should not be surprising, then, that American citizens from Forsythe County, Georgia, to Howard Beach and Bensonhurst in New York City interpreted the President's executive decisions as calls to action, which culminated in violence against minorities. From his denunciation of the Civil Rights Act of 1964 to his veto of the Civil Rights Restoration Act of 1988, Reagan demonstrated his contempt for minority peoples. These acts by the President were ostensibly aimed at so-called unconstitutional legislation in the first case and an attempt to free citizens from overbearing government in the latter. But the message citizens received from such behavior was that civil rights for minorities are not important and that virtually any sort of behavior, including anti-minority violence, is within the rights of white citizens. Or, as Chief Justice Roger B. Taney wrote in his *Dred Scott v. Stanford* decision in 1857, Blacks "were so far inferior that they had no rights which the white man was bound to respect."

Far too many innocent minority peoples have been victimized by whites. Protests almost always accompany such acts, but too many of them have been lost in history. It is hoped that by chronicling several recent cases from New York City, these fighters against injustice will not be forgotten.

Although the author is opposed to oppression wherever it exists, the attempt here is to deal specifically with anti-minority violence, especially acts committed against Black people in New York City during the Reagan/Koch era, beginning with the mass murder of Black men by Joseph Christopher in 1980 to the 1988 lynching of a Black teenager in Bensonhurst. The 1986 Howard Beach case is presented first because it exemplifies so well the racist climate and corrupt judicial system that characterized New York City during the 1980s. The Howard Beach case inspired many New Yorkers to engage in similar violent acts, and these too are recorded here. Greatest detail has been given to the highly publicized cases that ended in fatalities.

The focus of this book already has been criticized as "counter-productive" and "unbalanced" because it deals with a "narrow" aspect of the larger question of violence in U.S. society. (A broader treatment of this issue was, in fact, the subject of one of my earlier books, *The American Way of Violence,* Random House, 1972.) However, enlarging the book to include Black-on-white violence or Black-on-Black violence or violence in general would detract from the barely discussed but widely practiced phenomenon of white-on-Black violence. Those who are unhappy with this approach must turn elsewhere. It is the position of the author that this approach is legitimate and that the question of balance is irrelevant. Readers can decide for themselves whether such treatment is counter-productive.

Too often during the Reagan backlash years those in the vanguard of the struggle for social justice either were silenced or found it more convenient to apologize for or collaborate with injustice. Not so in this case. Unlike many minority analysts, the author is unwilling to remain silent or collaborate. The plight of minorities in American society stems not from something in their character, but from social arrangements designed to protect those in positions of dominance and sustain the subordinate status of minorities. The position taken here is that anti-minority behavior stems largely from racist attitudes, not from economics as some would maintain. While social class is an important consideration, it pales in significance when race is involved.

One of the most pronounced (and unfortunate) American character traits is the denial of bigotry. Such an attitude of deception only complicates the problem and renders its amelioration to the realm of the impossible.

Alphonso Pinkney
New York City, 1994

1

THE SETTING

New York is probably the most diverse city in the world, with inhabitants from every ethnic and racial group. The city-owned radio station, WNYC, at one time ended its daily program schedule with these words: "This is WNYC, New York City, where eight million people live in peace and harmony and enjoy the benefits of democracy." Fortunately, this practice ceased because there is neither peace nor harmony among the city's various ethnic and racial groups. Rather than being a traditional "melting pot" as some have insisted, New York is much more like a "pressure cooker," to use the words of former Mayor Robert F. Wagner.

It is true that many racial and ethnic groups co-exist in what might appear to be a form of cultural pluralism, but animosities between groups of people are always there and often explode into acts of hatred and violence, sometimes without provocation. Politicians know this, and they often exploit these feelings for their own purposes. By dividing

1

groups rather than uniting them (if that is possible), they are able to placate one at the expense of the other. This is clearly one way to keep the city divided and conquered.

Who were the people who comprised this, one of the largest cities in the industrialized world during the conservative 1980s? According to the 1980 census, more than seven million people lived within the five boroughs (counties) comprising New York City. These people lived within some 303 square miles. The boroughs range in population from 2.2 million (Brooklyn/Kings County) to .3 million (Staten Island/Richmond County). The borough of Queens (Queens County) had 1.9 million people; Manhattan (New York County), some 1.4 million people; the Bronx (Bronx County), 1.2 million people.

The population of New York City consisted of several ethnic and racial minorities in 1980, including some 1.8 million Blacks, 1.4 million Hispanics (Spanish origin), .25 million Asians and Pacific Islanders, and some 13,000 Native Americans. The Black population was largely made up of native-born people; however, a sizeable number of Blacks were from the Caribbean and Africa. The Hispanic people included nearly 1 million from Puerto Rico, along with large populations from the Dominican Republic, Cuba, Mexico and elsewhere in the Caribbean, Central and South America. The city had many white ethnic groups, but they are not identified as minorities by the census. Taken collectively, minority groups accounted for nearly one-half of the city's total population during the 1980s.

THE SETTING

Like most large American cities, New York is a city of ethnic enclaves. Even though the city is approximately half white and half non-white, it is not integrated. For example, a *New York Times* poll found that 72 percent of whites and 60 percent of Blacks lived in neighborhoods that are composed entirely or mostly of their own race.[1] But New York was less segregated as a city than others. Sociologists have developed what is called the "segregation index." If a city (or any other political subdivision) is either all-Black or all-white, the segregation index assumes a factor of 100. Conversely, if there is no racial segregation, the index is zero. During the 1980s, New York City's segregation index was 75, much lower than either Chicago (92) or Cleveland (91). The average segregation index of American cities of 100,000 -plus population is 81.[2]

The city's two major minority groups – Blacks and Hispanics – for the most part shared the same areas, but they tended to concentrate in particular parts of the city. The most populous borough, Brooklyn, was home to .75 million Blacks, who comprised about 32 percent of the population. There were some 400,000 Hispanics in Brooklyn, or approximately 17.5 percent of the population.* The remaining 1.2 million Brooklynites (some 56 percent) were white. In Queens, Blacks made up about 19 percent of the borough's population of nearly 2 million; Hispanics, more recent arrivals, accounted for 14 percent. The remaining 1.3 million (71 percent) Queens residents were white.

---

*Percentages do not add up to 100 because Hispanics may be of either race.

The borough of Manhattan was 22 percent Black, 24 percent Hispanic, and 59 percent white. In the Bronx, some 32 percent of the population was Black, 34 percent Hispanic, and 47 percent white. With .75 million people, Staten Island was the least densely populated borough with the smallest number of minorities. It had fewer than 10 percent Blacks and Hispanics combined. Whites made up about 90 percent of Staten Island's population.

Individuals of Asian and Pacific Island ancestry numbered nearly .25 million, and they were concentrated in Queens, Manhattan, and Brooklyn. The smaller populations (13,000) of Native Americans, Eskimos, and Aleuts were residents of Brooklyn and Manhattan.

Little attention has been paid to the demographic characteristics of the city's white ethnic groups (sometimes called ancestry groups), although they comprise a significant segment of the population and are certainly an important ingredient in the city's race relations. It is among some of these groups that the notion of "melting pot" is most relevant because many of them – the English, French, Germans, Italians, and Poles – are from multiple-ancestry groups, meaning that the present or past generations have married members of other ethnic groups.

During the 1980s, there were roughly fifteen major white ethnic groups in New York City, ranging from as few as 7,000 to nearly a million. By far the largest number of white ethnics were Italian or of Italian ancestry. With more than 800,000 people, they made up nearly one-third of the population of Staten Island, but a plurality of them lived in Brooklyn.

Following the Italians were the Irish, who numbered 318,000 in the city. They tended to concentrate in Queens, but a significant proportion lived in Brooklyn. They were exceeded in the population of Staten Island only by Americans of Italian ancestry.

Russians, both recent and earlier arrivals, comprised the third-largest white ethnic group in the city. They numbered over 200,000, mainly living in Brooklyn and Manhattan.

New Yorkers of Polish ancestry numbered nearly 200,000, with nearly half living in Brooklyn. People of German ancestry numbered more than 180,000, and nearly half of them lived in Queens. Residents of English ancestry (138,000) concentrated in Manhattan, while the Greeks (82,300) lived mainly in Queens.

People of Hungarian ancestry (64,000) lived mainly in Brooklyn, while those of French ancestry (32,000) overwhelmingly lived in Manhattan. Ukrainians (25,000) tended to live in Queens. Norwegians (15,000), on the other hand, tended to live in Brooklyn. People of Scottish descent (13,700) resided in Manhattan, while the Portuguese were likely to live in Queens.

Not many people of Swedish ancestry (9,600) lived in New York City during the 1980s, but those who did were most likely to live in Manhattan. The people of Dutch ancestry (7,600), like the Swedes, generally called Manhattan home.

Where white ethnics are concentrated in New York is in part an indication of length of stay in the country and also a function of economics. It also says something about their relative status in the larger society. Of the five boroughs,

5

Manhattan has the highest cost of living, and of the white ethnics living in New York City, the Dutch, English, French, Scottish, and Swedes were most likely to make that borough their home.

New York City during the 1980s had a population that was diverse in many ways: ethnically, racially, economically, educationally, occupationally, etc. Not unexpectedly, then, New Yorkers were divided in their attitudes in general and toward one another. Racial friction was pervasive, often manifesting as violence. Paradoxically, New Yorkers have a reputation of being somewhat more tolerant than Americans in other cities such as Chicago.

The presence of the United Nations, with missions from some 165 countries, gives New York an international flavor. Indeed, because of the UN, many people consider New York to be the "capital" of the world. However as many of New York's visitors have learned, compared to Amsterdam, London, Paris, or Stockholm, the city is more like a jungle than the cities from which they have come. The streets are full of homeless people, some of them suffering from schizophrenia. Handguns proliferate, and many are purchased or stolen with the express purpose of using them on other people. Thus, the rate of handgun homicides during the 1980s was vastly greater in New York City alone than in all of Western Europe.[3] While the likelihood of being shot was not as great as in some other American cities, the city's violent crime rate was a high one.

THE SETTING

. . .

Writing about Harlem in 1965, Kenneth Clark assessed it and other Black communities in the United States as follows:

The dark ghetto's invisible walls have been erected by the white society, by those who have power, both to confine those who have no power and to perpetuate their powerlessness. The dark ghettos are social, political, educational, and – above all – economic colonies. Their inhabitants are subject peoples, victims of the greed, cruelty, insensitivity, guilt, and fear of their masters.[4]

In the 1920s and 1930s, Harlem was known as the "capital of the Black world." Without a doubt it is still the most famous Black community in the United States. Situated in the borough of Manhattan, Harlem's boundaries are 90th Street to 178th Street and the Harlem and Hudson rivers. In the mid-1980s, Harlem's population numbered some 250,000 people.

According to the New York Convention and Visitors Bureau, Black people from Lower Manhattan began moving north into Harlem in 1910, the "indirect" result of the construction of the city's subway. The Harlem Visitors and Convention Association maintains that Blacks were "obliged" to leave midtown Manhattan because of the construction of Pennsylvania Station. While both of these rationales contain some truth, the development of Black Harlem was somewhat more complex.

At the turn of the present century, New York City had a population of some 61,000 Blacks scattered throughout the five boroughs, and most of them lived in Manhattan. These citizens worked at a variety of low-status jobs, most of them in domestic

7

service occupations. Because of the high death rate among Blacks, their population remained relatively stable throughout the second half of the 19th century. The high death rate was caused by infant mortality, pneumonia, and tuberculosis.

The Black population of Manhattan lived among other working-class immigrant and indigenous people, but invariably they lived apart from the others; many streets and blocks were largely Black. Toward the end of the 19th century, most Blacks lived in two sections of mid-town Manhattan known as San Juan Hill and the Tenderloin. These two contiguous sections stretched from the 20s to the 60s on the West Side, with the Tenderloin having the largest population. This section, after several name changes, is called Clinton today.

The Black population of New York City was constantly fed by migrations from the South and immigration of others from the West Indies. This movement, especially that from the South to the North, continued unabated until the beginning of World War I. Racial violence in the South was responsible for much of the migration, especially in the last decades of the 19th century and the first decade of the 20th, but many Blacks left in search of economic opportunities. Industrialization spurred rural Blacks and whites alike to come to the cities in search of work, which most Blacks found in factories that needed unskilled laborers.

Blacks who came to New York found that in employment they were relegated to the lowest status positions. Those who did not do menial work in factories were forced to work as domestic servants. Likewise, those fleeing racial violence were in for a rude awakening: racial violence in New York City was widespread. In all aspects of life, Blacks were subjected to segregation and discrimination. According to historian Gilbert Osofsky, "The attitudes of New Yorkers wavered with national trends of racial adjustment."[5] At times, the city was considered to be tolerant; at other times, attitudes were rigidly racist.

Although civil rights legislation was passed in New York State to protect the rights of minorities in public transportation, theaters, and restaurants, it did little to change the racist attitudes of white New Yorkers. Despite their ethnocentrism and internal clashes, white ethnics were in complete agreement on one key point: as a "race apart," Blacks were perceived as innately inferior to whites. Such views were regularly published in newspapers and magazines, some of them by white immigrant clergymen.

While there were several reasons for the movement of Blacks from Manhattan to Harlem, a major race riot in 1900 certainly must rank as a major impetus to this relocation. On the evening of August 12 of that year, a Black man left his apartment on West 41st Street to buy cigars for friends in a nearby bar. In the early morning hours of August 13, the woman with whom he lived went to the corner in search of him. While awaiting him she was approached by a white plain-clothes policeman who charged her with "soliciting." The Black man approached the scene to find the policeman using

9

force to arrest the woman. He interceded. The policeman clubbed him and shouted racial epithets, whereupon he pulled out a knife and slashed the policeman. The Black man escaped from the city, while the policeman, the son-in-law of the captain of the local police station, died in a hospital the next day.

This incident was followed by several others in the next few days. According to Osofsky, "The entire neighborhood went wild with rage." Blacks in the Tenderloin were attacked by mobs of racist whites. White street gangs, long a feature in the Tenderloin, systematically beat up all the Blacks they could find. The police made no effort to curb the anti-Black violence; indeed, they often led the mobs. When not leading the mobs, the policemen simply attacked all Blacks they could find.

It took a severe rainstorm on August 16 to end the seemingly endless violence, which had filled area hospitals to full capacity. Orders went out from the local police to keep Blacks off the streets, and soon the Tenderloin returned to the precarious state that had existed before the riot. Although white mobs indiscriminately beat numerous Blacks and killed two of them, as so often happens in the United States, it was Black people who ended up in jail.

The major newspapers in New York were quick to criticize the police and white citizens for their violence, but they showed little sympathy for the Black victims. A grand jury charged with investigating the riot refused to indict a single policeman on the grounds that accusations were brought against groups, not individuals. But when cases were presented against individual policemen, they too were dismissed. In its year-end *Annual Report*, the Police Department concluded that New York City had been threatened with a race war, but that "Prompt and vigorous action on the part of the police" had kept the riot under control. Realizing that they could not live peacefully, albeit on a segregated basis, Blacks took advantage of the opportunity to move north to Harlem.

Prior to 1900, Harlem had been home to some of New York's wealthiest and most famous families. It became home to newly arriving Irish and Italian immigrants who lived in shanties along the banks of the river. The wealthy, on the other hand, lived in large estates, rows of brownstones, and exclusive apartment houses equipped with elevators and servants' quarters.

One of the turning points in Harlem's history occurred when the elevated subway train was extended into the area. Speculators then began coming to this desirable neighborhood. They made fortunes buying land, holding it for a short time, then reselling it. Blacks were not new to the area; some had worked as slaves on the nearby farms and large estates. Indeed, among the first Blacks to settle there were the servants of New York's wealthy. As in the Tenderloin, Blacks in Harlem at the turn of the 20th century lived in segregated slum areas.

The land speculation business caused too many houses to be constructed in Harlem. This forced property owners to rent and sell to Blacks, usually at higher prices than they could expect from whites. Thus, Harlem became home to ever-increasing numbers of Blacks. Because this was the only area where they could live in relative peace, by the end of the first decade of the 20th century there were some 50,000 Blacks living in Harlem. Blacks were not welcomed by whites; indeed, restrictive covenants were enacted to keep them out. But because white property owners were unable to rent all of their property to whites, they were forced to rent to Blacks.

As a result and in a fashion so typically American, Harlem became virtually all-Black by 1920. Whites eagerly left the area, and Blacks from the South flocked there. By 1930, more than 160,000 Blacks lived in Harlem, many of them from states bordering the Atlantic Ocean – Virginia, North and South Carolina, Georgia, and Florida.

In the relatively short period of one decade (1910-1920), Harlem was transformed from what some had called an ideal community into a slum. Primarily responsible for this transformation was the high cost of housing and the low salaries of Black wage earners. The houses and apartment buildings in the area were originally built for the wealthy, and thus were much too expensive for unskilled Black workers to maintain. Developers eventually carved up the buildings into multiple-unit complexes. This led to the creation of one of the largest, most congested slum areas in the city, if not the country. For example, the Civil Rights Commission reported in 1959 that, "if the population in some of Harlem's worst blocks obtained for the rest of New York City, the entire population of the United States could fit into three of New York's boroughs."[6]

In 1964, a group of community leaders and professionals

known as Harlem Youth Opportunities Unlimited (HARYOU) published a lengthy report on the Harlem community called *Youth in the Ghetto*. HARYOU was primarily concerned with the deteriorating conditions of the community and their impact on its citizens. Insofar as housing was concerned, this report showed that the Harlem community contained twice the proportion of overcrowded housing units than did the city as a whole. In New York City, some 85 percent of the housing was defined as "sound," while half of the units in Harlem were so classified. The other half were defined as "deteriorating" (in severe need of repair) or "dilapidated" (unsafe and inadequate shelter).[7]

Such housing has had deleterious effects on physical health as manifested in increased rates of acute respiratory infections, childhood infectious diseases, and home accidents. Indeed, HARYOU discovered that Harlem had a much higher crude death rate than did the city as a whole, with an infant mortality twice as great. Deaths from such preventable diseases as pneumonia, tuberculosis, and influenza were also double that of the city as a whole.

In addition to poor physical health, the Harlem community was characterized by massive social problems. For example, the rate of juvenile delinquency at the time was more than twice that of the city as a whole, and the rate of narcotics addiction was considered to be among the highest in the country, with nearly one-half of some categories of addicts living in the community. Furthermore, Harlem served as the source of narcotics for much of New York City and the entire metropolitan area.

The living conditions in Harlem were also directly related to the venereal disease rate. It was reported that the rate of venereal disease among youth under 21 years of age in Harlem was 110 per 10,000 residents while the rate for New York City was only 17 per 10,000. In addition, poor economic and living conditions forced a disproportionate segment of the Harlem population to rely on public assistance. At the time of the HARYOU study, one-third of all persons under 18 years of age in Harlem were recipients of Aid to Families with Dependent Children. For New York City, the rate of children in the same category was less than one percent.

In Harlem, the homicide rate was startling: six times as great as that of New York City. Among young Black males, homicide was the leading cause of death, exceeding accidents by a considerable margin.

These social problems, caused in part by substandard living conditions, lack of economic opportunities, and other inequities, have made today's Harlem a community of massive problems that have directly impacted the quality of life of community residents. Furthermore, the problems are responsible for the widespread emigration from the region. In the decade from 1950 to 1960, for example, the population of the community declined by more than 10 percent.[8] Many of those who stayed would no doubt leave today if given the opportunity. It should be added, however, that many community residents remain because they know that Harlem is still one of the few areas in New York City where Blacks can live in relative racial peace; others remain because of a strong identification with the community and its cultural institutions.

. . .

The race riot of 1900 was only one of the many random acts of violence against Blacks. During the colonial period, especially during slavery, the city's so-called free Blacks were forced to live amidst regular acts of racial violence at the hands of the local white population. One of the more massive acts occurred in 1863 in what became known as the Draft Riots. When white longshoremen went on strike for higher wages, they were replaced by Black workers. And when these striking whites were drafted to fight in the Civil War, they objected to serving in a war to free Blacks. Their resistance took the form of massive acts of violence, usually directed toward Blacks. In July 1863, whites randomly attacked Blacks, killing persons and destroying property. When the war ended in 1865, the violence continued.

The period immediately following the Civil War was an especially violent one, not unlike the 1980s. President Lincoln's successor, Andrew Johnson, who assumed office in 1865, could be considered a precursor to Ronald Reagan. During the period of Reconstruction, adopted policies geared toward returning Blacks to the slavery conditions that had prevailed before the Civil War.[9] In the 1980s, Reagan took positions strikingly similar to Johnson's. The executive decisions of both men created an atmosphere in which acts of racial violence thrived throughout the country.

President Johnson sanctioned white home rule in the South, turning responsibility for Reconstruction over to the same people who had fought to retain slavery. Congress enacted the Freedman's Bureau Bill, which was designed to aid refugees and freedmen by furnishing supplies and medical services, establishing schools, and leasing or selling to them confiscated or abandoned lands. Also, Congress enacted the Civil Rights Bill. Johnson vetoed both bills – the Freedman's Bureau Bill because it was "unconstitutional" and proposed to do for Blacks more than ever had been done for whites, and the Civil Rights Bill because, he believed, Blacks were not ready for the privileges and equalities of citizenship. The attempt by Congress to override his veto of the Freedman's Bureau Bill failed. But on April 9, 1866, Congress passed the Civil Rights Bill over his veto. Shades of April 1988! Furthermore, Johnson had condemned the proposed Fourteenth Amendment.

Congress also voted to override President Johnson's veto of the Reconstruction Act of 1867, a bill that was designed to divide the South into military districts in which martial law was to prevail. On the basis of universal suffrage, a convention in each state was to draw up a new constitution acceptable to Congress, and no state was to be admitted to the Union until it ratified the Fourteenth Amendment. Johnson believed that the bill was unconstitutional, unfair to states, and that Blacks did not understand the franchise. Although Reagan's language was not as blunt as Johnson's, his actions were quite similar. And they gave impetus to the random violence against Blacks.

Although Blacks enjoyed a degree of freedom during the decade of the Reconstruction (1867 to 1877), the struggle for equality was far from over, and violence against them continued. The Supreme Court had already ruled in the 1857 Dred Scott decision that people of African descent were not and could not be citizens of the United States, and that they had "no rights which white men are bound to respect." In 1896, it added to the notion of Black inferiority in the *Plessy v. Ferguson* decision, ruling that separate but equal facilities for Blacks did not violate the Constitution. Separate facilities for Blacks remained part of the American Way of Life up through 1954.

Persons in leadership positions, especially the president and members of the Supreme Court, must not understand how their actions and pronouncements give credence to anti-Black violence – but this is difficult to believe. Blacks and others in New York City understood that the anti-Black statements made by Mayor Edward Koch led to increased tension between groups in the city. His racist statements during the 1988 presidential primary in New York, especially his vicious attacks on Jesse Jackson, the first serious Black candidate for President in American history, caused consternation among leaders and citizens of the city. His comment that Jews and other supporters of Israel would have to be "crazy" to vote for

17

LEST WE FORGET: WHITE HATE CRIMES

Jesse Jackson was considered by most New Yorkers to be nothing more than a racist attempt to defeat the candidate and a move to generate racial hostility among New Yorkers.

Throughout much of the history of the South, racial violence most often took the form of lynching. Thousands of Black people, mostly males, met gruesome deaths at the hands of lynch mobs — often while men, women, and children picnicked or otherwise celebrated the event. The police would either side with the mob or turn their heads the other way.

Lynching usually stemmed from rumors of a crime by Blacks against whites, not infrequently a rumored rape of a white woman by a Black male. Many, if not all, of these rumors were based on false allegations, incorrect identifications, or outright lies. Lynching became a means of keeping Black people in their place, and for many of the mobsters, that meant keeping Black men away from white women. These grotesque acts, most of them public, had the effect of demoralizing and terrifying Black people. While the number of tree hangings has diminished, lynching took a different form during the 1980s in New York City. It is difficult to know whether a Black man discovered hanging from a tree in Central Park in 1987 was the victim of a racist mob or whether his death resulted from some other source. There is no doubt, however, that the deaths of Michael Griffith in Howard Beach and Yusuf Hawkins in Bensonhurst at the hands of white mobs were the functional equivalents of lynching.

Lynchings were never as characteristic of the North as

they were of the South. Outside the South, race riots could be considered the northern equivalent to lynching. These mob acts of violence were largely urban and served to instill fear in Black people. Historically, they have been the source of death for thousands of Blacks, killed simply because they were Black.

Race riots were often the work of white ethnic groups who, it is said, were in competition with Blacks for economic opportunities. Such behavior was not characteristic of all white ethnic groups, whether competing with Blacks or not. And they certainly were not solely the work of poor whites, no matter how much middle-class whites might make that claim. Both lynch mobs and race riots were led by whites of all socio-economic strata, as the mob attacks in Howard Beach and Bensonhurst clearly demonstrate. In the end, they were much more racial incidents than those originating from social class.

The role of law enforcement officers has been critical in both lynchings and race riots. White police officers usually supported whites in cases of racial violence. Black victims were often made available to white mobs on demand (or polite request) by police officers, sheriffs, and other law enforcement officials. And even if the police did not participate, they often encouraged the mob.

The civil rights laws and court decisions of the 1950s (*Brown v. Board of Education*, 1954) and the 1960s (the Civil Rights Act of 1964 and the Voting Rights Act of 1965) led many Americans to assume that America's racial problems would soon be solved. That has not been the case; indeed, it now appears that whatever progress had been made was eroded in the 1980s.[10] The most alarming trend was the resurgence of overt racist behavior. It somehow became acceptable to openly express negative attitudes toward racial minorities, especially Blacks. Ethnic jokes were a staple in offices around the country, and racial violence was rampant.

In 1988, a commission of political, business, education and civic leaders, including former presidents Jimmy Carter and Gerald Ford, issued a report in which they described how the United States has been regressing in its efforts to promote equal opportunity for minority groups. This report found that in "education, employment, income, health, longevity and other basic measures of individual and social well-being, gaps persist – and in some cases are widening – between minority groups and the majority population."[11] One of the many findings of the commission was that median income of Black families rose from 54 percent of the median white family income in the 1950s to 61.5 percent in 1975, but then fell to 57.5 percent by 1985. So much for the myth that race was not the dominant variable in American life for Blacks and other minorities.

Findings of this report are noted here because, more than the resurgence of racial violence, the continued denial of equality to minorities is, beyond doubt, the most serious problem the society faces, both domestically and in its relations with a polarized and ever-changing world. And as the behavior of citizens reflects the actions and philosophies of policymakers and other leaders, it should come as no surprise that the declining governmental commitment to minority equality and increasing racial violence are but two sides of the same coin. This is no mere correlation; the former causes the latter.

2

RECENT SURGE OF

RACIAL VIOLENCE

More than anything else, the 1980s will be remembered as the decade during which amorality reigned supreme. Many words have been used to describe this syndrome that Ronald Reagan, more than any other person, installed as the pinnacle of the American Way of Life. Greed, meanness, narcissism, selfishness, apathy, insensitivity, and intolerance characterized this unfortunate decade. During the 1980s, "freedom" meant free enterprise run wild, and one was rewarded for faithful adherence to the notion that *what* one got was far more important than *how* one got it. It was clearly within "ethical" bounds to exploit others savagely to achieve monetary success.

The 1980s saw the increasing number of millionaires keep pace with the increasing number of homeless Americans in cities, suburbs, and rural areas. Intolerance for people who, by virtue of birth (that is, by ascriptive criteria), were distinguished from the "social elite" ran rampant among the upper economic classes. Virtually any treatment of these people has been viewed as fair game. Indeed, their plight is seen as a blemish on an otherwise just society.

Railroad commuters come into New York City from the sanitized suburbs of New York, Connecticut or New Jersey through Grand Central and Pennsylvania Stations, where one either steps over or avoids the homeless en route to an office in a gaudy building on Wall Street or Madison Avenue. The homeless are perceived as lazy, not exploited by an economic system designed to make the rich richer with little regard for the less fortunate. The first inclination of the amoral Americans is to ignore the plight of the homeless. This ignorance is then transformed into irritation and hatred, such as when restaurant owners lace their garbage with rat poison to keep these unfortunate people away.

When Ronald Reagan commenced his campaign for the presidency, conservatism was emerging as the dominant ethos of the society, and it encompassed all aspects of social life, especially attitudes toward and treatment of members of ethnic and racial minorities. It was no accident that Reagan began his campaign in Philadelphia, Mississippi, the town that became infamous throughout the world as the site of the murder of three young civil rights workers – James Chaney, Andrew Goodman, and Michael Schwerner – by members of the Ku Klux Klan in 1964. Reagan's gratuitous act signaled the beginning of a

24

successful campaign and two terms in office that can only be characterized by the eradication of the gains made by minorities, especially the civil rights of America's Black population.

Throughout his presidency, Reagan made it clear that he held only contempt for Black people and their aspirations. Although a largely disengaged and unattached chief executive,[1] he made it clear to all that, as an ideological conservative, he was determined to return the country to the stage that existed prior to the New Deal administrations. While Reagan did not always directly supervise all policy decisions, his associates were well aware of his ideological positions. This enabled them to deduce his stance on any particular issue.

Reagan's public position on civil rights for minorities and women was quite reactionary. In addition to his opening campaign speech in Philadelphia, Mississippi, he let it be known that he was opposed to the Voting Rights Act, the Equal Rights Amendment for women, economic sanctions against South Africa, abortion rights for women, and many other so-called liberal issues.

The litany of Reagan's insults against Black people is quite long. He opposed the Civil Rights Act of 1964 on the grounds that it was an unconstitutional infringement on private property rights. He reconstituted the Commission on Civil Rights, filling it with people who were opposed to civil rights for minorities and women. Under his direction, the Commission would eventually close down its offices around the country.

It will probably come as no surprise that Reagan opposed legislation making Martin Luther King Jr.'s birthday a national holiday; he said it was inappropriate and would prove too costly. Moreover, the Reagan Administration introduced and supported legislation allowing tuition tax credits to private schools that discriminated against minorities.

When Congress voted to impose economic sanctions against the apartheid government of South Africa (the Anti-Apartheid Act of 1986), Reagan vetoed the bill, which was later passed over his veto. In similar fashion, Reagan vetoed the Civil Rights Restoration Act of 1988, which would have restored and expanded some of the provisions that the Supreme Court had limited in a 1984 ruling. Again, the House of Representatives and the Senate overrode the veto.

Finally, in what can only be called a bizarre news conference regarding South Africa's ban of all multiracial, non-tribal organizations opposed to that government's policy of racial separation, Reagan said, "It is a tribal policy more than a racial policy." Such ignorance was both ridiculous and dangerous.

For eight years, Ronald Reagan opposed every legislative initiative and judicial decree designed to advance minority rights. This caused some people to question his sincerity when, during a trip to the Soviet Union in April 1988, he lectured the Russian people on human rights while opposing minority and women's rights and ignoring the massive problem of homelessness in the United States. The Russians understood that his was a message of anti-communism rather than one of peace and justice.

By his public stance, Reagan made it clear to all, especially to those who worked in his administration, that civil rights for minorities was not an important issue, that indeed, he *opposed* greater civil rights, especially for Blacks. Such an attitude, within a general climate of intolerance, had the effect of unleashing the forces of prejudice in the society and making overt acts of racism acceptable in a way that had not been the case for more than two decades. The point is that *Ronald Reagan set the tone and created the environment in which acts of racial violence thrived.* Although the climate of opinion in this area might have found support without his direct encouragement, the president's public positions on issues of civil rights assured that overt racism would thrive. Reagan's position was so influential that white college and university students throughout the country no longer felt the need to conceal their attitudes on race.

It would not have mattered much if the attitudes of younger people remained negative toward minorities. However, in this climate of disdain for minority rights, other white Americans opted to translate racist attitudes into behavior. Thus, the widespread physical attacks on Blacks and other minorities went unchecked.

Ronald Reagan managed, without much difficulty, to bring out the very worst in the American character. It was not only white people or the man on the street who succumbed to the culture of amorality. Whites *and* Blacks in positions to shape public policy contributed their share. A group of Blacks who themselves had profited from affirmative action programs joined in this movement of neoconservatism, abandoning the very Blacks who had made their advancement possible. They supported the conservative administration at home and abroad, backing such anti-communist policies as the American interventions in Central America and Angola, the invasion of Grenada, and the bombing of Libya. At home they opposed affirmative action for women and minorities, supported the movement to abolish the minimum wage, and generally opposed the government's role in assisting citizens incapable of supporting themselves.

Even though some of the Black neoconservatives called themselves social democrats, their policy recommendations were compatible with those of the radical right. In so doing they constantly offered apologies for racism. For example, Black sociologist William Julius Wilson has maintained that gains in the struggle against poverty must depend on the private sector, not the government.[2] Furthermore, he believes that the struggle of Blacks in the United States is no longer a function of racism, for race is no longer a salient variable in our newly emerged "color-blind" society. Such pronouncements at a time when racism and racist attacks have escalated is little more than an attempt to blame the victims of oppression for their own social status.[3]

Whether they know it or not, Black neoconservatives are contributing to the oppression of other Blacks and lending support to the racist attacks on Black people. For example, some of these people saw fit to support the racist subway vigilante Bernhard Goetz in his unprovoked shooting of four Black teenagers on a New York subway in December 1984. Roy Innis, the director of the Congress of Racial Equality (CORE), made pronouncements supporting whites against Blacks whenever there was a racial confrontation in New York City. Such behavior earned him the praise of Ronald Reagan and others hostile to the legitimate aspirations of Black people and prominence on national television news programs.

The behavior of these Black apologists raised remarkably little outcry in the Black community, largely because those who differ are denied access to the public media, and those who manage to persevere in the struggle against oppression are simply dismissed. The Black neoconservatives are the Booker T. Washingtons of the 1980s, America's equivalent of South Africa's Black collaborators.

One of the lessons to be learned from this period in American history is that conservatism is, by its very nature, racist. This explains the dearth of Black people in the Republican Party. While Republicans gave lip service to the recruitment of Blacks, those in the inner circles of the White House spent their time making derogatory jokes about minorities. Former Secretary of Education Terrell Bell reported that while he was a member of the Reagan cabinet from 1981 to 1984, racist jokes were the order of the day. He said that the slurs included references to Martin Luther King Jr. as "Martin Lucifer Coon," to Arabs as "sand niggers," and to Title IX of the Civil Rights Act, which guarantees equality for women in education, as the "lesbians' bill of rights."[4] Such slurs from "midlevel right wing staffers" at the White House and the Office of Management and Budget were commonplace, Bell recalled.

One of the more candid and honest evaluations of Ronald Reagan's presidency, especially his actions on civil rights, came from Justice Thurgood Marshall, the first Black to sit on the United States Supreme Court. When asked in a television interview to evaluate the civil rights records of various presidents, past and present, Marshall said that Reagan was at "the bottom" of the list. "Honestly, I think he's down with [Herbert] Hoover and that group – Wilson. When we [Blacks] really didn't have a chance," Marshall noted.[5] The response of the president was that his record on civil rights had been "outstanding."

Certain characteristics distinguish human beings from other forms of animal life. These characteristics comprise what is called "human nature," and one of the essential features of human nature is the ability to empathize with others in times of tragedy. If one watches the news on television and sees members of a family in some jungle thousands of miles away grieving because of some tragedy, the tendency is for human beings to empathize and somehow share their grief in sadness rather than ignore it with laughter. When human beings are unable to empathize with others, regardless of culture, they have either failed in the process of socialization or they simply regard the victims as less than human beings. This is because all human beings are born with the capacity to empathize with others. People who have been improperly socialized often kill brutally, as witnessed in these recent incidents from New York City: people were pushed off a subway platform in front of on-rushing trains; subway change booths were fire-bombed, killing the clerks; homeless people have been set ablaze; a shopping bag lady was raped and strangled. Where is the reverence for life, the most sacred of human values?

Clearly, the perpetrators of racial and ethnic violence do not view their victims as human beings, for they display not even a remote sense of remorse. Jon Lester, the chief initiator of anti-Black violence in Howard Beach, watched Michael Griffith die as he was flung many feet into the air by an automobile. Clearly, Lester did not equate himself as a fellow human being with the deceased; indeed, in the midst of this tragedy, he turned and viciously attacked Cedric Sandiford with a baseball bat. During the months of the trial, Lester showed no remorse, nor did his family or friends. He was less concerned about his Black victims than had the tragedy happened to a pet dog.

Insofar as racial violence is concerned, part of the American character has always dictated that Black people be viewed as subhuman. This practice dates back to the days when Blacks were officially declared "non-human" in the Constitution during the era of slavery, thereby permitting the most gross acts of violence against them. When Christians decided that they could no longer justify human slavery in view of their religious teachings, they evaded the issue by stating that Blacks were not human beings. And later, the 20th-century "lynching parties" in the South clearly demonstrated the criminals' perception of their Black victims as inhuman. Such thinking became entrenched in the early days of this nation's history and is widespread today. The Jon Lesters of today are continuing a longstanding tradition initiated by their ancestors.

That the incidence of racial violence actually increased after the racist lynching in Howard Beach indicates that there is no dearth of white people who perceive Blacks as less than human. While some people saw the 1980s as a time for racial reconciliation and engaged in such activities as interracial visits, others seized the opportunity to give overt support to their deeply held racist views. The New York Police Department reported, for example, that there were 76 incidents of racial violence in the city during the first month after the Howard Beach attack.[6]

The nature of the brutality inflicted on Black victims is particularly outrageous upon close examination. The policemen who murdered Michael Stewart and Eleanor Bumpers at close range and who felt no guilt for their acts obviously do not see Black children, young people, or grandmothers as people like themselves. The same can be said for the white civilian murderers of Willie Turks, Michael Griffith, and Yusuf Hawkins. And how can a *human being* murder another and then cut the victim's heart out, as did Joseph Christopher? Such behavior at close range is qualitatively different from the murder of hundreds of thousands of human beings in Hiroshima and Nagasaki from 35,000 feet via airplane, or the destruction of whole villages in Vietnam by dropping anti-personnel weapons and napalm from airplanes. It is not, however, unlike the murder of thousands of Vietnamese men, women, and children who were perceived by American military personnel as "gooks" (not human beings) who deserved their fate.[7]

Closer to home, in New York City and elsewhere in the U.S., teenagers have been known to douse homeless persons with gasoline, ignite them and then watch them experience a painful death.

There seems to be little doubt that in the United States, there are many persons, including many teenagers, who have not been properly socialized into what we normally call human beings. While it is true that widespread use of drugs, especially crack, seems to transform some people into walking monsters, it is also true that the socialization process has failed many.

The New York City Police Department and the City Commission on Human Rights both established units to report on what are called "bias incidents" in the city. These are crimes considered to be motivated by race, ethnic background, religion, or sexual orientation. The Bias Incident Investigating Unit was created in 1980. In September 1987, this unit reported a "significant" increase in racial assaults in New York City, especially following the mob attack in Howard Beach. But police officers insisted that racial tension was not necessarily increasing; rather, they maintained, the high numbers were probably a function of more accurate reporting.[8] Although there are guidelines for reporting bias incidents, there is little agreement on how to define them; thus, cases are frequently reclassified. Clearly, many incidents that were bias-related were never classified as such. The police officer in charge of the bias unit, Inspector Michael Markman, said of the rash of racial attacks after the Howard Beach case, "We see isolated, spontaneous, random types of attacks or incidents."[9] To New York's Black residents, however, these attacks represented systemic and planned ongoing brutalization by whites.

The former Commissioner on Human Rights, Marcella Maxwell, whose Bias Response Team's work consisted mainly of working with community leaders in specified neighborhoods, attributed the rash of racial attacks to housing segregation, which they claimed prevented citizens from getting to know each other. But the truth is that these incidents of racial violence stemmed from the lack of a commitment to equality, as manifested by many acts of the Reagan Administration, not the least of which was a callous disregard for affirmative action and other policies geared to making racial peace and justice.

It was ironic that the New York City Police Department had major responsibility for investigating bias incidents because police officers were often charged with the very acts they were ostensibly investigating. (This is the functional equivalent of putting Dracula in charge of a blood bank.) In 1983, when the first Black Police Commissioner, Benjamin Ward, was appointed, the head of the Patrolmen's Benevolent Association (the police union) said in a television interview that he had no immediate comment on Ward's appointment because he needed time to adjust—meaning, of course, that members of the department had never served under a Black police commissioner. At the very time of the Howard Beach attack, several white police officers were facing charges of killing Blacks.

Of the 29,000 officers in the New York City Police Department in 1987, Blacks and Hispanics accounted for 11 percent each. This in a city where Blacks made up more than 25 percent of the population and where Hispanics accounted for about 20 percent. The difference between those at the bottom ranks and those who held higher status positions was even more striking: Black officers held 3.4 percent of lieutenant positions; only 1.9 percent were captains. Hispanics held even fewer of the high status positions: 2.1 percent were lieutenants and 1 percent were captains.[10]

Minority policemen themselves have often been the victims of disparaging remarks. Indeed, white police officers often directed such remarks toward Commissioner Ward! For example, when Mayor Koch spoke at a Patrolmen's Benevolent Association convention in September 1987, he was repeatedly interrupted with chants of "Where's Bubba?"[11] At the same convention, representatives of the major ethnic associations within the department were announced and cheered by the crowd. But there was no mention of the Guardians, an internal organization comprised of 2,500 Black officers. When asked about the convention, an official of the Guardians said they had not attended because of hostility from white officers. "Every time we would send someone there, they would boo or make derogatory remarks," he said.[12]

When asked whether he thought the Black commissioner's presence had led to smoother race relations in the department, Roger Abel, president of the Guardians, said that having a Black commissioner had "little impact" on the daily experience of Black officers at the precinct level. One of the major recommendations of the 1968 National Advisory Commission on Civil Disorders called for "the recruitment of additional black officers, and for the review of promotion policies to ensure fair promotion of Negro officers."[13]

The police have become known for authoritarian behavior, one of the manifestations being racial bigotry.[14] It seems highly unlikely that their attitudes toward minorities are any different from the general population; perhaps they are simply more rigid. Many police officers either deliberately elect an occupation in which force is an integral part, or they become more steeped in bigotry from working as police officers. There appears to be no limit to the lengths they will go to maintain the oppressed status of minorities. In urban areas in particular, police officers follow a widespread practice of carrying toy guns to plant on their victims, who are often killed, so that they can claim the killing was in self-defense.[15]

During the 1980s, one of the most widespread of all discriminatory practices committed by the police was perjury.

As some of the cases in the following chapters will demonstrate, the police simply refused to testify against a fellow officer, even though they might have witnessed the officer committing appalling offenses. The practice of police perjury was widespread and led to cover-ups of crimes in which minorities have been killed or maimed by police officers. Adding to this practice, juries invariably refused to convict police officers of murder, although all available evidence pointed to cover-ups — as in the well-publicized cases of Michael Stewart and Eleanor Bumpers. This practice is sometimes called the "wall of silence."

While punishment is theoretically a function of the courts in this society, police officers often assumed the duties of other agencies in the criminal justice system, especially with regard to the summary execution of minority citizens. As the society continues to become ethnically and racially more heterogeneous, however, it is possible that the presence of more minority and female police officers will serve to diminish police abuse of power.

The increase in cases of racial violence, especially in New York City, came as a surprise to some people. It was rather widely believed that the civil rights gains of the 1960s and 1970s would serve to diminish racial violence. But with the Ronald Reagan backlash, the reverse proved to be the case. As soon as the conservatives assumed power, overt racism again became part of the norm of the society.

LEST WE FORGET: WHITE HATE CRIMES

The administration of Ronald Reagan will probably be judged by future historians as the one that went to extreme lengths to reverse the rights that minorities and women had achieved as a result of years of struggle. But throughout his years as president, Ronald Reagan remained one of the most popular of all American presidents. Even those who claim they have suffered because of his policies are likely to express their admiration for Reagan. Coming to the presidency after the United States's defeat in Vietnam, Americans longed for a leader who would again inspire patriotism. Although frequently criticized in newspaper editorials and columns as a president known for mis-statements, flights of fantasy, a corrupt administration, scandals, official lawlessness, and sleaze in general, he remained popular with the American people. That in itself says something about the character of United States citizens.

The Reagan backlash appealed to many closet racists. Newspaper and magazine writers frequently abandoned any cloak of objectivity and joined him in his anti-communist and racist crusades. Many magazines (e.g., *Commentary* and *The New Republic*), once known as liberal journals, completely abandoned this position and joined the backlash bandwagon. Articles they published in the 1980s would have had few, if any, outlets in the 1960s. Black neoconservatives, dormant a decade ago, suddenly emerged, lending support to Reagan's policies. Conversely, more moderate or progressive voices found themselves without outlets. In some cases Black neoconservatives used such gimmicks as class analyses as cover-ups for their own anti-Black racism. Compassion and decency became characteristics labeled as old-fashioned and even un-American.

It should come as no surprise, then, that racial violence thrived in such a climate. Violent outbreaks are simply manifestations of the American character that give expression to long-held beliefs about Black inferiority. Those who thought that the civil rights legislation of the 1960s and 1970s signaled the end of the bloody confrontations between Black and white citizens had erroneously assumed that equality in principle also meant justice in practice. Such was clearly not the case.

Virtually any behavior, cloaked in the guise of anti-communism, is fair and desirable, both at home and in the world, especially the Third World. The American government, through the Central Intelligence Agency, has been involved in drug trafficking at least since the beginning of the Vietnam War.[16] The drug "problem" in the U.S., according to many politicians and others, is the most serious issue facing the society. Yet, one agency of the government (the CIA) pushes drugs on the population, while another (the Drug Enforcement Agency) is charged with waging war on drugs. The enormous profits from drugs are used to support wars against women and children in the Third World. And ruling at the height of the CIA's drug pushing was one George Herbert Walker Bush.

Ever since World War II, the government of the United States has engaged in wars, always against Third World countries, and almost always against "progressive" regimes.

The United States has intervened in countries throughout the world in an effort to "contain communism," beginning with Korea and continuing in Guatemala, Lebanon, Cuba, the Dominican Republic, Vietnam, Angola, Grenada, Nicaragua, Afghanistan, Libya, and Panama. These wars have made American citizens virtually immune to violence, and since they were all conducted against people of color, it is understandable that anti-minority racial violence is so widespread. When lip service is paid to reverence for human life, it means, to most Americans, reverence for white lives, not those of minorities.

Meanwhile, on the home front, Black children, grand-mothers, and others continue to be victims of racist killings and attacks throughout the country. In no other city has such behavior been more pronounced than in New York, long considered a melting pot, a city characterized by racial toler-ance. The number of incidents of racial violence in the past 15 years has served to at least partially dispel these myths. In the years following the racist mob murder of Michael Griffith in Howard Beach, literally hundreds of racial attacks have been recorded. The situation reached the point where Black people and members of other minority groups were afraid to leave their places of residence. It became dangerous for them to sit in public parks or to ride the subway, to say nothing about being caught in neighborhoods where white ethnics predominate. New Yorkers had heard about Cicero and Gage Park in Chi-cago, but it never occurred to them that Gravesend and Bensonhurst in Brooklyn and Howard Beach in Queens were also forbidden territories for Blacks. They were in for a rude awakening.

It is impossible to say with certainty that the mass acts of racial violence that occurred in the United States during the 1980s and afterward can be traced directly to the Reagan Administration's policies, but one can certainly make the case that they are related. After all, the perception of what a government is willing to tolerate is important in determining the behavior of citizens.

.   .   .

Attention is now turned to several of the many acts of anti-minority violence in New York City during the 1980s, years when Ronald Reagan served as president of the United States and Edward Koch was mayor of New York City.

3

MICHAEL GRIFFITH: HOWARD BEACH*

OVERVIEW

Howard Beach has become synonymous with anti-Black prejudice, and rightfully so, given the family and community support of the young toughs who, without remorse, chased one Black man to his death and, while he was dying, then turned to his companion and brutally beat him. Scenes in Howard Beach were reminiscent of the southern lynch mobs gathered to celebrate the lynchings of Black men. The attitudes of the residents were hardly different from those of lynch mobs. Both were intensely prejudiced against Blacks and other people of color.

Howard Beach is an isolated and insulated community in the borough of Queens, near Kennedy International Airport. It is bounded either by water or a wildlife refuge on three sides.

---

*All references for Chapters 3-10 are listed in the Reference Notes section following Chapter 11.

Prior to 1956, the community was serviced by the Long Island Railroad, but the subway was extended to it in that year. The community is surrounded by three nearby shopping malls that permit the residents to exist independent of New York City. These factors give Howard Beach the character of a small town.

Only two percent of Howard Beach's population is minority, and they live a precarious existence in the midst of racial hatred. The majority residents, on the otherhand, boast about the ethnicity of their neighborhood. One 16-year-old student at Stela Maris High School, Michelle Napolitano, told a reporter, "We're strictly a white neighborhood. They [the Blacks involved in the attack] had to be starting trouble." Another resident, 52-year-old Carol Vandezee who grew up in the neighborhood, said, "This is a predominantly White and Italian neighborhood. We have had break-ins and robberies, but never any racial murders."

The more than 18,000 residents of Howard Beach are not ashamed of their bigotry. While in the 1970s and 1980s other predominantly white neighborhoods in Queens and elsewhere in the area became racially and ethnically integrated, Howard Beach has strongly resisted the entrance of others into the neighborhood. For example, in 1971, the residents resisted the construction of a public housing project in the neighborhood, forcing the construction of the development to be cancelled.

In New York City, the Open Housing Center maintains a file of complaints by minorities who have been denied housing. In 1986, there was one complaint from Howard Beach, this by a Hispanic man who was attempting to purchase a home. In an interview, the director of the Open Housing Center said, "They've created almost a barricade around their little world. What Black would want to move into that mess? You see what happened [meaning the racial attack] and you can't believe it's 1986 and you can't believe you're not talking about South Africa."

Black people, especially those who live in the adjacent neighborhoods, are well aware of the racism of Howard Beach's residents. The president of the Jamaica New York branch of the National Association for the Advancement of Colored People, June Van Brackle, said, "Our people won't even drive through Howard Beach unless it's the last resort. There's just an innate bad feeling you have about the place." Reverend Timothy Mitchell of Flushing, Queens said, "Howard Beach is a place where Blacks don't like to go. They know the hostility and virulent racism there."

Comments by residents present a picture of this racist community: "Puerto Ricans and coloreds have no business here after 8 P.M. The [white] kids had no right to start trouble, but the Black men never should have been here," said Julio Breviario, a wallpaper hanger. Speaking of the police assigned to guard the home of the defendants who were cooperating with the police investigation, 12-year-old Louie Porcelli said, "There are cops all over the place, and that's good and bad." He was asked, "Why good and bad?" "I want them around, but when the cops aren't there any more, they're going to come around and start trouble," he replied. When asked who "they" were, a friend replied, "the eggplants," while another said, "the Melanzane." At that point Porcelli said, "the coloreds." He was asked how he felt about the death of the Black man in the racial attack. "I was sad until I found out the guy was high on coke." (Defense attorneys maintained that Michael Griffith had used cocaine shortly before the attack.) These attitudes expressed by children clearly reflected the views of their bigoted parents.

Howard Beach is a community serviced by the 106th police precinct – the same precinct in which Black men had been tortured with electric stun guns (four white policemen served time in prison for these crimes). It is also a community that serves as home to organized crime figures, and there have been several gangland murders there. One of the community's best known and respected residents is John Gotti, the reputed head of the Gambino crime family.

Perhaps the incident that best illuminates the racism of Howard Beach occurred during the march to protest the attack and killing of Michael Griffith. The demonstration took place two days after the December 22 attack. Organized by civil rights leaders, the march was to protest the attack and also to demonstrate that the streets of the community were not a white preserve. As the group of Black (and several white) demonstrators arrived in the Howard Beach community, they were met by a mob of local whites who chanted, "Niggers go home," "Tribes go home," "Go back to Africa," and "KKK and Howard Beach."

Thirty cars of Black demonstrators descended on the New Park Pizzeria, the site of the attack, and staged a noisy demonstration. It was reminiscent of demonstrations that took place in the deep South in the 1960s when Blacks protested segregated restaurants.

Given the racism prevalent in Howard Beach, it was not surprising that a bloody attack would occur that fateful night of December 20, 1986, an attack even New York's mayor, long known to be unsympathetic to the aspirations of Black people, called "a racial lynching." He said, "This is the most horrendous incident of violence in the nine years I have been mayor. We have 1,800 murders a year in this city and they're all bad, but this is the worst murder I believe that has taken place in the modern era." True to form, however, he later denounced one of the victim's actions as worse than the lynching when Cedric Sandiford, complaining of police harassment, initially refused to cooperate with the investigation.

THE ACCOUNT

According to police officers, and their version has been verified by others, on December 20, 1986, four Black men went from their home-base in Brooklyn to Queens to pick up one of their paychecks. The 1976 Buick in which they were traveling broke down on an isolated stretch of Cross Bay Boulevard in Queens. Three of them, Michael Griffith, 23, Timothy Grimes, 20, and Cedric Sandiford, 36, walked to find a public telephone to summon assistance while the fourth, Curtis Sylvester, 20, the owner of the car and an out-of-town relative of Griffith who was visiting for the Christmas holidays, remained in the vehicle.

They walked three miles to the New Park Pizzeria at 156-71 Cross Bay Boulevard in Howard Beach.

Around the same time, some 30 white youths were attending a birthday party for Steven Schorr, 18, at his home at 156-48 80th Street in Howard Beach. For entertainment they had hired a stripper called "Bendetoo" (alias Edna Bennett, alias "Cindy the Cop") to perform for $115. The performance began at midnight.

At around 12:30am, Jon Lester, 17, William Bollander, 17, and Salvatore DiSimone, 19, left the party to drive Claudia Calogero, 16, and Laura Castagna, 16, home. On the way, they encountered the three stranded Black men walking on Cross Bay Boulevard. Lester and his group yelled racial insults as they continued to drive. After dropping off Calogero, they returned to the party, where Lester announced to the others, "There are some niggers in the pizza parlor. We should go back and kill them."

Twelve white teenagers left the party in three cars looking for the three Blacks. In addition to Bollander, DeSimone, and Lester, Harry Buonocore, 18, Thomas Farino, 16, Thomas Gucciardo, 17, Scott Kern, 18, Jason Ladone, 16, Michael Pirone, 17, James Povinelli, 16, Robert Riley, 17, and John Saggese, 19, all went on the hunt.

They went immediately to the pizzeria, arriving at about 12:40am. When they encountered the Black men, they yelled, "Niggers, you don't belong here." They chased and beat the men, who were trying to escape.

Both Griffith and Sandiford were caught outside the pizzeria. The police charged that Jon Lester beat the men with a baseball bat, Scott Kern used a tree limb and Jason Ladone punched with his fists. During the beating, Sandiford said to Jon Lester, "My God, I have a son like you, 17-years-old. Please don't kill me!" In response, Lester, who at the time was facing a gun possession charge, smashed him across the face with the baseball bat. The remaining two Black men, Timothy Grimes and Curtis Sylvester, broke away from the mob and ran as they were pursued for seven blocks. When they arrived at a wooded area, they were again beaten by the mob.

Timothy Grimes did manage to escape. He ran north on Cross Bay Boulevard and hitchhiked to Brooklyn. He approached a car with two white women who had parked to telephone police about the Black man (Cedric Sandiford) whose body they had seen on the highway. He asked, "Could you give me a lift? A lot of people are chasing me." They did not give him a ride, but he managed to hitchhike a ride to Brooklyn, thereby saving his life.

Michael Griffith managed to get away, diving through a hole in the fence along Cross Bay Boulevard. Cedric Sandiford pretended to be unconscious for a few minutes until the attackers left in their automobiles. He was later picked up by a police car. Farther along Cross Bay Boulevard and pursued by the angry mob, Griffith was forced onto the Shore Parkway section of the Belt Parkway, a busy six-lane highway, where he was struck and killed by a car driven by Dominick Blum, a 24-

year-old officer in Manhattan's Family Court. Prior to the accident, Blum, his girlfriend, Martine Channon, and another friend had attended a play at Brooklyn College and had dinner at a local diner. They left at about 11:30pm to drive Blum's and Channon's friend home to Flushing. Upon their return to Brooklyn at about 12:30am, while Channon was asleep in the car, Blum maintains that the break lights of the car in front of his suddenly flashed red. He looked over his shoulder prior to moving into another lane. While looking back, he says that Michael Griffith came over the median barrier and directly into the path of his car.

The car struck Griffith with full force, propelling him onto the hood, where his weight cracked the windshield and sent his body 20 feet into the air. When he landed, his skull was crushed. Cedric Sandiford later maintained that Blum was a part of the mob that attacked him. Blum insisted, however, that he did not know the people responsible for the attack. Furthermore, Blum thought he had hit either a tire or an animal. He drove to the home of his parents in Flatbush, Brooklyn. His father, a New York City police officer, accompanied him back to the scene of the accident about an hour later, when Blum maintains he learned that he had killed someone for the first time.

After chasing Griffith to his death and beating both Sandiford and Grimes, the white teenagers returned to the party. Jon Lester, who returned with a baseball bat, was overheard saying boastfully, "One got killed, one got away, and one got beat up." Later, a group of the attackers returned to the parkway in two separate cars. There they saw three police cars on the side of the parkway. Salvatore DeSimone said to the others, "See, I told you the Black guy got killed." Clearly, the white teenagers felt no remorse about what happened.

The police found Michael Griffith's body around 1:00am. Gwen Harlodman, an assistant medical examiner, reported that he died of "multiple fractures of the skull, pelvis and extremities with internal injuries to the brain and aorta with hemorrhage." The examiner also found a "fibrous encapsulated projectile – a .25 caliber bullet – lodged in the right side of Griffith's chest."

Some of the participants and observers of the attack talked openly about the brutality. For example, attacker Thomas Farino claimed that he tried to persuade the Black men to leave the neighborhood, and as he was talking to them, "Jon Lester ran up behind me and started hitting Sandiford with the bat." Jason Ladone, another attacker, maintained that when Sandiford attempted to escape from the beating, "I punched him a couple of times. Tommy Gucciardo began kicking him." Scott Kern said, "I ran up and found Tommy Farina on 156th Avenue trying to stop Lester from hitting the Black guy on the back of the legs with a stick. I didn't do anything."

Two residents of the area, Angelina Romanillos and her sister Theresa Fisher, were at home when they heard screaming. They looked out of the window and saw a Black man being chased by several whites. When they went to the front door they saw Cedric Sandiford being beaten. They called the police emergency number and reported that 12 whites were beating three Blacks with a tire iron near 156th Avenue and 86th Street. A dispatcher informed police that the beating was taking place at *84th* Street. Fisher got into her car and drove through the neighborhood looking for Sandiford so that she could assist him.

George Toscano was visiting in Howard Beach when he heard dogs barking. When he went to the door he saw several whites surrounding Sandiford, one of whom hit him in the stomach with a baseball bat. Toscano's wife dialed the police emergency number. When she did not get an answer, she hung up.

George Boos was driving along the highway when he saw a human figure jump over the divider. Then he saw the figure hit by a dark car. He stopped his car, went over to the splattered body, knelt down and felt for a pulse, but there was none. He then encountered a white teenager who made several derogatory remarks about Blacks. He left the scene before the police arrived.

At around 1:00am, two police officers, Steven Braille and Ronald Siegel, both of whom were patrolling the area, were asked to respond to an accident. When they arrived on the scene, several vehicles, including an ambulance, were already there. A tall Black man (Cedric Sandiford) approached, knelt over the body and said, "Oh my God. This is Michael."

The police were questioning Sandiford when the Blums arrived at the scene. Dominick Blum informed the police officers that he was the driver of the car that hit Griffith. He maintained that he did not know what had happened, and was not arrested by police. The police maintained that he could not be charged with leaving the scene of the accident because he returned to the scene. However, state traffic law requires that a driver who strikes a pedestrian stop and report the accident to authorities as soon as possible. Blum agreed to testify before the grand jury without immunity.

A Queens grand jury voted on May 21, 1987, to not bring charges against Blum because of insufficient evidence. On November 2, Blum was summoned to testify in the trial of those charged with the racial attack. It was only after he returned with his father to the scene of the accident that he learned what had happened, Blum testified. Defense lawyers, however, sought unsuccessfully to portray Blum as responsible for Griffith's death, an effort to vindicate their clients of murder.

The authorities treated Blum with considerably more compassion than they did the Black victims. After he returned to the scene with his father, he was permitted to return home without being charged. He was not tested for alcohol or night blindness. Rather than focusing on the actions of Blum, the police elected to devote their energies to scrutinizing the Black victims, whom they continued to treat with suspicion.

Cedric Sandiford, who had been badly beaten by the mob, was dazed when he was interviewed by the police shortly after Michael Griffith's death. While trying to explain what had happened, one of the officers pushed him, spread-eagled, against the patrol car, took off his coat and started frisking him. Sandiford angrily told them that he was the victim of a crime, not the perpetrator. He was informed that, as a matter of policy, the police search everyone they put into a patrol car. Once inside the car, the officers questioned Sandiford for three hours, his wounds remaining untreated until he was finally taken to a hospital.

Because of the insensitivity with which Sandiford was treated and because Sandiford's lawyers were unhappy with the way the case had been handled by Queens District Attorney John Santucci, Governor Mario Cuomo was asked to appoint a special prosecutor to take over the case. When Cuomo initially refused to appoint a special prosecutor, Sandiford and his lawyers refused to participate in the investigation. The lawyers for the victims accused Santucci of "bad faith" and a "cover-up" in the inquiry. However, they said they would cooperate if the case was taken over by a special prosecutor.

Meanwhile, three days after the initial attack, three white teenagers – Scott Kern, Jason Ladone, and Jon Lester – were charged with second-degree murder in the case. The police reported that a tip led them to the home of one of the accused and that he implicated the others. Upon their arrest, Santucci's office maintained that Griffith's death resulted from "depraved indifference to human life." Kern, Ladone and Lester were arrested and held without bail, and the police announced that additional arrests could be expected.

However, the charges of murder, manslaughter and assault against the three teenagers were thrown out by Queens Judge Ernest Blanchi on December 29, citing insufficient evidence. He let stand charges of reckless endangerment. During these hearings in Queens Criminal Court, Cedric Sandiford refused to testify.

Mounting world-wide publicity finally prompted the governor, after three weeks of indecision, to announce at a news conference with Black leaders on January 13, 1987, that he had agreed to appoint a special prosecutor, Charles Hynes, to the case. Temporarily relieved of his duties, Hynes would devote all of his efforts and time to the Howard Beach case and any other cases growing out of it. Santucci voluntarily relinquished his jurisdiction in the case. Black leaders expressed satisfaction with the decision, for Hynes had developed a reputation as a tough but fair lawyer. He had successfully headed major criminal investigations into police corruption, medicaid fraud, and racketeering. Lawyers for the victims agreed to cooperate fully with Hynes.

On January 20, 1987, Hynes commenced presenting evidence to a Queens grand jury. Two weeks after testimony and evidence, the grand jury voted criminal indictments against the 12 youths involved in the racial attack. The indictments included murder charges and several lesser ones. The three charged earlier – Kern, Ladone, and Lester – were named in the new indictments. Three of the 12 were charged with murder, and the nine others were charged with lesser crimes. Scott Kern, Jon Lester, and Robert Riley were charged with second-degree manslaughter and assault, in addition to murder. According to the indictment, the three "acting in concert" caused the death of Michael Griffith "under circumstances evincing a depraved indifference to human life" which caused him to run onto the Belt Parkway "and thereby caused his death when he was struck and killed by an automobile."

The investigation into the case was facilitated when one of the teenagers, Robert Riley, came forward to cooperate. Riley's action prompted the special prosecutor to recommend that he be released without bail. According to Hynes, Riley came to his office, accompanied by his lawyer and his parents, and was told of the harsh alternative he might face at a trial if he did not cooperate with the investigation. Soon after, he agreed to cooperate. His cooperation provided valuable information about the attack and helped to identify and secure indictments against the 11 others. Because of his cooperation with the investigation, Riley was permitted to plead guilty to assault, and the charges of murder and manslaughter against him were dropped.

Rather than praising Riley, the residents of Howard Beach attacked him for turning on his friends. Two police officers had to be stationed at his home 24 hours a day. He stopped attending John Adams High School and was tutored at home. In addition, he was forced to quit his after-school job as a delivery person for a local pharmacy.

The 12 participants in the racial attack were from either working-class or middle-class families. With the exception of Jon Lester, they were all residents of Howard Beach. All were between 16 and 19 years of age at the time of the attack. They were either close friends or casual acquaintances.

THE PERPETRATORS

William Bollander was forced to drop out of John Adams High School after suffering a stroke. At the time of the attack, he was attending night school and was to have taken the high school equivalency test. He was charged with riot and inciting to riot.

Harry Buonocore was a student at Pace University, majoring in management. In high school he had been an honor student. He was charged with riot.

Salvatore DeSimone was a sophomore at Pratt Institute in Brooklyn, majoring in communications design. He worked part-time for a beer distributorship. DeSimone was charged with riot and criminal facilitation.

Thomas Farino worked at Tony Roma Restaurant on Cross Bay Boulevard and was a junior at Christ the King High School when the attack occurred. Farino was charged with riot.

Thomas Gucciardo graduated in June 1986 from Archbishop Molloy High School. His father was an engineer, and his mother was a school teacher. Gucciardo was charged with attempted murder, assault, and riot.

Scott Kern was a junior at John Adams High School. He is the third of four children and worked part-time pumping gas. Harold Kern, his father, worked as a meter inspector for Consolidated Edison. Kern was charged with second-degree murder, manslaughter, attempted murder, assault, riot, and conspiracy.

Jason Ladone was a junior at John Adams High School. His father was a city sanitation worker. Landone was charged with attempted murder, manslaughter, assault, and riot.

Jon Lester was a junior at John Adams High School. He also worked part-time as a counter person at the Lindenwood Diner. He said that he wanted to be a mafia capo when he finished high school. Lester moved with his parents and three siblings four years ago from Manchester, England, to Florida, where they opened a restaurant. Following a divorce, Jean, his mother, brought the children to New York. At the time of the indictment, Lester was a prisoner in protective custody at Downstate Correctional facility in Fishkill, where he was serving time for a gun possession charge. Lester was charged with second-degree murder, manslaughter, attempted murder, assault, riot, and conspiracy.

Michael Pirone had attended John Adams High School but dropped out and took a job at a trucking company. He was in physical therapy at the time of the attack, the result of a hit-and-run automobile accident that left him with two broken legs, two broken arms, and a broken jaw. Pirone was charged with manslaughter, assault, and riot.

James Povinelli was planning to attend St. John's University beginning in 1987, but his father died shortly after the racial attack. He then took over his father's knife sharpening business. He was the sole source of support for his mother. Povinelli was charged with riot.

Robert Riley was a senior at John Adams High School. His father was a corrections officer at the prison ward of Kings County Hospital. Riley is the youngest of four children. His brother was a New York City police officer. Riley was charged with second-degree murder, but charges were reduced to assault when he cooperated with the investigation.

John Saggese was a freshman at St. John's University, having graduated from Archbishop Molloy High School. He worked part-time in a delicatessen on Cross Bay Boulevard. He was charged with riot.

THE VICTIMS

Michael Griffith, the second of five children, was a construction worker from Brooklyn. He came to New York as a boy from Trinidad and later graduated from Prospect Heights High School. His mother, Jean, worked as a nursing assistant. He was the step-son of Cedric Sandiford. Michael Griffith was planning to be married.

Timothy Grimes was an unemployed construction worker at the time of the attack.

Cedric Sandiford, Michael Griffith's stepfather, has worked as a mechanic's assistant and construction worker. Born in Guyana, he served two years in the United States Army. During the attack, he was beaten severely with a baseball bat, tree limbs, and other weapons. He was treated at Jamaica Hospital and released, but his injuries rendered him unable to work for at least one year.

Curtis Sylvester, a Tampa, Florida resident and owner of the car that stalled, was a student at Florida State University. He was Michael Griffith's cousin.

THE TRIAL

The Howard Beach attack came at a time when New York's Black population had been victimized by many racial attacks. Although the Howard Beach beatings received more publicity than any of the others, it was no more brutal than the murders of Willie Turks, Michael Stewart, Eleanor Bumpers, or the other victims detailed in this book.

In the period between the indictment and the trial in the Howard Beach case, opponents of racism charged that the President of the United States was in large measure responsible for the climate of race relations in the country. That is, they asserted that the Reagan-led conservative backlash, with its contempt for the civil rights of Blacks, had created a climate of racial hatred in the country. In his attack on Reagan, Presidential candidate Jesse Jackson said, "When people have health care and jobs to share they tend to be more generous, but when they are losing those things they have nothing left but race to focus on. It is almost a setup to pit working-class Whites against poor Blacks when both are two sides of a devalued economic coin."

New York City's Black police commissioner Benjamin Ward, not known as an outspoken critic of racism, called the Howard Beach attack and others a function of the President's reactionary policies with regard to civil rights. He claimed that it was Reagan's policies that "have built up the kind of [racial] tension that we're seeing in this city today." He maintained that there had been progress in civil rights "up until the time of the election of President Reagan. And then I believe that intentionally or unintentionally – I choose to believe it was intentional – a whole series of things were done in Washington that I think gradually built up that tension and exacerbated it."

Several protest marches led by Blacks, were held to demonstrate that streets and public places in all neighborhoods are open to all people. While demonstrating in Howard Beach, Canarsie, and the Bath Bay sections of Brooklyn, the marchers were met with shouts and signs: "Niggers go home," "White power," "KKK," "Tribes go home," "Back to Africa," and "Bring back slavery." Black demonstrators also held several city-wide "Days of Outrage" activities to protest racial violence. In one such demonstration, protesters managed to disrupt rush-hour traffic by blocking bridges and halting traffic on eight different subway lines. The activities of hundreds of thousands of commuters and shoppers were disrupted for hours.

Mayor Edward Koch continued his customary anti-Black stance by disagreeing with the police department's report on the number of racially motivated attacks. The department reported that bias-related violence had increased in the city, and that Blacks were most often the victims. Koch characteristically said that no matter what the statistics showed, whites were more often the victims than Blacks, "When a Black is a victim, it's racial," he declared. "And when a White is the victim, it's robbery." Since declaring upon his election as mayor that "Blacks are anti-Semitic," Koch persisted in demonstrating to New Yorkers his contempt for Blacks right up until the day he was defeated by David Dinkins. As Vernon Mason, a civil rights lawyer and leader of the "Days of Outrage" demonstrations, has said on many occasions, "Ed Koch is the chief architect of racism in the city."

. . .

As the trial of the first four defendants approached, the Medical Examiner's office reported that traces of cocaine had been in Michael Griffith's body when he was killed. Defense attorneys for the attackers maintained that the cocaine indicated that perhaps these "weren't three innocent people walking along who were just standard motorists, but there may have been some instigation on the part of these three people to cause the confrontation." While the amount of cocaine was described as "low to moderate" by the Medical Examiner's toxicology report, the defense lawyers continued to pursue the issue throughout the trial.

In the meantime, Cedric Sandiford filed suit against the City of New York for $25 million, asserting that police had conducted a bad-faith investigation and that they failed to protect him adequately.

Of the 12 people indicted in the Howard Beach case, Scott

Kern, Jason Ladone, Jon Lester, and Michael Pirone were to be tried first. They had been charged in the indictments with committing felonies, including second-degree murder, manslaughter, attempted murder, and assault.

The lawyers for the defendants, known for their defense of so-called underworld crime figures, made it known prior to the trial that they would treat the victims as criminals. They maintained that the attack had not been racially motivated, that the death and beatings resulted from a confrontation in which the Black men were the aggressors looking for a fight and that Michael Griffith's death was an accident for which the defendants were not responsible. They claimed that the three Black men had been armed with knives and possibly guns. The defense lawyers were Gabriel Leone (for Scott Kern), Bryan Levinson (for Jon Lester), Stephen Murphy (for Michael Pirone), and Ronald Rubinstein (for Jason Ladone).

Judge Thomas Demakos was at one time a policeman. He was also the prosecutor in the case in which police officer Thomas Shea was charged with murdering 10-year-old Clifford Glover in Jamaica, Queens on April 28, 1973. Demakos was born in Manhattan and raised in the Bronx. He received a bachelor's degree in accounting from Long Island University and degrees in law and business administration from New York University. In 1962, he became a member of the Queens District Attorney's office, in part because the Archbishop of the Greek Orthodox Church insisted that the District Attorney appoint a Greek American assistant.

During jury selection for the Howard Beach trial, it was obvious to all involved that the defense attorneys did not want Blacks, or any other people of color, to sit in judgement of the white mob. After two weeks of jury selection, the special prosecutor in the case, Charles Hynes, charged that defense lawyers were operating under the presumption "that Blacks, because of their race and for no other reason, would have a different perception of justice than would other jurors." Because of this, he maintained, defense lawyers were deliberately keeping Blacks off the jury. At this point, six jurors had been chosen, and they were all white.

At issue in the case presented by the special prosecutor is the peremptory challenge, during which a lawyer may disqualify a limited number of prospective jurors without giving any reason. In this case, three prospective Black jurors had been peremptorily dismissed from the jury panel. Lawyers usually use the peremptory challenges to exclude jurors whom they feel may not be favorable to their side. In addition to peremptory challenges, lawyers are allowed an unlimited number of challenges "for cause," but reasons for such actions must be stated.

It is a widespread practice throughout the country that in cases where Black people are involved, Blacks are systemically rejected for jury duty simply because they are Black. In 1986, the United States Supreme Court ruled in *Batson v. Kentucky* that prosecutors cannot use their peremptory challenges to dismiss potential jurors simply because they are Black. In this decision, Associate Justice Thurgood Marshall wrote in a concurring opinion that "Misuse of the peremptory challenge to exclude black jurors has become both common and flagrant." In political subdivisions around the country, even in places where Black people predominate, many trials involving Blacks end up before all-white and often bigoted juries. But the court did not address the constitutionality of the peremptory challenges when they were employed by a defense lawyer rather than a prosecutor in the Howard Beach trial.

In the Howard Beach case, the special prosecutor argued that the judge should apply to the defense the same restrictions as the Supreme Court applied to prosecutors in the *Batson* ruling. He argued that Supreme Courts in California, Florida and Massachusetts have held that neither the defense nor the prosecution may use peremptories to exclude Blacks as a group.

Judge Demakos ruled on September 21 that defense lawyers were indeed seeking to exclude Blacks from the jury, and that he would curb the lawyers' challenges against prospective Black jurors. Defense attorneys moved to appeal the ruling, and jury selection was temporarily halted. Judge Demakos' ruling was the first in New York State that held that defense lawyers were improperly using peremptory challenges to keep Blacks from a jury.

Judge Demakos declared in his ruling that "from the totality of circumstances of the case, including the observations made by the court, a prima facie case has been made" that the defense lawyers were "using their peremptory challenges to strike jurors on the ground of group bias alone." He said he would extend to the defense lawyers the Supreme Court ruling that prohibits prosecutors from engaging in such practices. In the Howard Beach case, each side in the trial had 20 peremptory challenges, and each side had used five. The judge said he would order defense lawyers to give nonracial explanations whenever there were "any further allegations that they were exercising peremptory challenges against Black jurors on the ground of group bias alone."

The defense lawyers appealed the ruling, but the Court of Appeals refused to review it. This led to the seating of one Black juror. When jury selection was completed, the panel included, in addition to the one Black juror, six whites, two Hispanics of Puerto Rican ancestry, two Asian Americans, and one man from Guyana with Asian roots.

In his opening statement to the jury, the special prosector claimed the three Black men had pleaded with the white mob for mercy and that one of the victims was "mercilessly chased" to his death on a busy highway, another savagely beaten. He said that the victims were attacked by the mob simply because they were Black.

In their opening statements to the jury, defense lawyers accused the prosecution of building a case based on the accounts of perjurers and other untrustworthy witnesses and on the false view of the Black men as victims when they were the aggressors. Brian Levinson, one of the lawyers said, "You will have to decide whether they were three lambs walking into Sodom or whether they were three antagonistic men spoiling for a fight, looking for trouble and coming across some youngsters."

When Curtis Sylvester testified, the defense attorneys commenced their campaign to show that the three Black men involved in the attack were unsavory people who had been the aggressors in the confrontation with 12 white teenagers. Sylvester was grilled on the following issues: whether Griffith or Sandiford had knives during the attack, whether or not he was involved in drug trafficking, and whether the Black men had gone to Queens to buy drugs.

One of the most striking aspects of the trial was the vociferousness and provocative way in which the defense lawyers questioned prosecution witnesses. For example, when Theresa Fisher, who is white and who witnessed the attack from the home of her sister in Howard Beach, was testifying, she tearfully exclaimed that the defense lawyers were "getting me upset." She was also provoked to anger on several occasions. Such questioning caused Judge Demakos to warn the defense attorney that he was "going to have the Queens County Bar Association monitor [his] conduct during the course of [the] trial." The impression the defense attorneys sought to convey was that Fisher was lying, and that as a white person she had no business testifying against fellow whites.

Perhaps the most severe questioning by defense lawyers came when Timothy Grimes took the witness stand. He was so badgered by defense attorney Stephen Murphy that he left the witness stand before the questioning was over, shouting obscenities at Murphy saying, "I'm getting out of here." During a recess in the trial, Michael Griffith's brother Christopher said of Grimes, "He cried today in my arms." In addition to Murphy's interrogation, Grimes left the witness stand because of the behavior of the four defendants. They were laughing wildly as Murphy asked one hostile question after another. Murphy continued his drive to paint Grimes as an unsavory person, dwelling on his past record as though it was relevant. The defense attorney suggested that Grimes had used money meant for his girlfriend's children to purchase crack and other drugs for himself, that he had lost six jobs since 1982, that he relied on others to buy his clothing, and that he had run away from Howard Beach, leaving Sandiford and Griffith to fend for themselves.

Before he cross-examined Grimes, Murphy told reporters, "I can't wait. I'm going to break him. You'll see." And after he finished he said, "I set out to get him rattled and let his true personality come through." During one of Murphy's "improper" questions, Frank Ladone, the father of one of the defendants, was ejected by the judge for applauding. The courtroom, it seemed, had turned into a trial of the victims of the attack. Indeed, lawyers for the victims in the case filed a complaint with the Grievance Committee of the Appellate Division of State Supreme Court. The complaint charged that Murphy "repeatedly and incessantly harassed, argued with and viciously attacked prosecution witnesses . . . in transgression of legal rules of evidence and procedure."

Perhaps the prosecution witness most disliked by the defense was attacker Robert Riley, who had agreed to cooperate with the prosecution in return for a reduction of the charges against him. His testimony was considered by the prosecution to be the most crucial of the trial. When he was asked if he had cooperated with the prosecution in order to avoid a prison term of 25 years to life if convicted, Riley said, "When I saw how serious it was, I had to do something for the wrong I did." He testified that he had consumed 10 to 12 cans or bottles of beer in two-and-a-half hours at the party. This prompted one of the defense attorneys to say that Riley was so drunk at the time of the attack that his account could not be trusted.

Even when Jean Griffith tearfully told the jury how she had gone to the morgue to identify her son's body, the defendants and their families showed no remorse. Griffith wept as she described what was left of her son's battered body.

When Cedric Sandiford was called to the witness stand to testify, he said he had been beaten with bats and tree limbs by the mob as they chased him and his companions through the streets of Howard Beach. "They were beating me all over my body, my back, my legs, my stomach, everywhere," he said. He mentioned that he had begged one youth to stop beating him, saying that he had a son about the same age as the attacker. Rather than stop, the mobster "lashed me in the head and busted my head open and blood was running down the back of my neck. I felt like my brains had busted apart." When asked if the attacker was in the courtroom, he said yes and pointed to Jon

Lester, who had admitted to a detective that he had beaten Sandiford.

During the hostile, combative questioning, one of the defense lawyers asked Sandiford how many steps he had taken between the time he left the pizza parlor and the time he spotted the white mob. Sandiford exploded, "They attacked me, sir! They came at us, sir! They said, 'niggers, get the fuck out of the neighborhood!'"

After six weeks of testimony by 60 witnesses, the prosecution rested its case in the Howard Beach trial. The defense lawyers said that none of the defendants would be called to testify but refused to give reasons for this decision. In keeping with their contention that the victims were the aggressors in the case, one of the defense lawyers maintained that Michael Griffith was responsible for his own death. "He caused his own death. He had many ways to go" and did not have to dash onto the parkway. They also presented, as an "expert" witness, a toxicologist who had not participated in the autopsy and who testified that Griffith's decision to run onto the parkway could have been a misjudgment resulting from the effects of cocaine.

Defense attorney Stephen Murphy argued that when the white youths approached the victims, whom he claimed were displaying knives, the mobsters "wet their pants and stood there and did nothing." He said they had left the party, driven by "the old macho garbage." He maintained that "racism [had] nothing to do with this trial. The truth of the matter was that it [Griffith's death] was an accident brought about by stupidity."

In their closing arguments, the defense attorneys claimed that their clients committed no crimes, that the attack was caused by the Black men who were unsavory characters, and that politicians were exploiting the Howard Beach attack.

In his closing argument, Special Prosecutor Hynes declared that a gang of teenagers yelling racial epithets in a "night of fists, fear, terror and hatred" chased a Black man into a "chasm of death" during an attack on the three victims. According to Hynes, the attempt by the defense to shift blame for the attack was a mere smokescreen.

Hynes then attacked the defense lawyers for attempting to portray the victims as unsavory people who were looking for trouble when they entered Howard Beach. "No matter how the lawyers for these defendants try to destroy the reputations" of the Black men, "they had a right to walk through the streets of Queens County and did not need a passport to get into Howard Beach." Pointing to the defendants and noting that even though they were dressed like young men who might be attending their high school graduation, he asked the jurors to envision the way they looked on December 20th – "faces twisted with hate, yelling filthy racial epithets and threats of violence."

POST-TRIAL REACTIONS AND SENTENCING

The jury received the case on December 10, 1987, three months after the trial commenced, and announced its verdict on December 21, after 12 days of deliberations. Jon Lester, Scott Kern, and Jason Ladone were found guilty of second-degree manslaughter and first-degree assault; but Lester and Kern were both acquitted of second-degree murder. In addition, Lester and Kern were also found guilty of conspiracy. Michael Pirone was acquitted of manslaughter, riot, and assault. This verdict turned on the distinction between depraved indifference to human life, as required for a murder conviction, and reckless indifference, sufficient for a convictionn of manslaughter.

Needless to say, the verdict was interpreted differently, depending on whether one was Black or white. The Commissioner of the New York State Division of Human Rights, Douglas White, said, "I think there is a real feeling in the Black community that justice was not done because there was no murder conviction. Blacks are going to be looking very, very closely at the sentences."

Mayor Koch said, "It seems to me to be a responsible verdict that was not racially motivated." Manhattan's Borough President David Dinkins said he thought the verdict demonstrated that there can be justice, but "I would have been happier if we had gotten murder in the second degree in the case of Kern and Lester."

The congressional representative for the district in which Howard Beach is located, Floyd Flake (a Black man), said he felt the verdict was a fair one, all factors considered. He said the process had been fair, regardless of the decision. Representative Charles Rangel claimed that the jury's decision demonstrated that "Whites cannot take the law into their own hands and disregard the safety of citizens because of the color of their skins."

Assemblywoman Geraldine Daniels, who represents Harlem in the state assembly, said the verdict demonstrated that "equal justice under the law is possible in New York City and New York State." The editor of the *Amsterdam News*, Wilbert Tatum, on the other hand, called the verdict "a profound disappointment. There are no redeeming features in it at all. It just shows how cheaply Black life is regarded in this city."

The president of the New York Urban League, Harriet Michel, claimed she was gratified by the decision, "But the larger issue in this city is the fear that every Black citizen must feel that they could suffer injury at the hands of the police or the majority community just based on their color." She continued, "And I find it a sad commentary on the system that many Blacks feel that to get a conviction on any charge is more than they had hoped for." As the director of the New York City Council of Churches attested, "I think the manslaughter charge is a good verdict. In my wildest hopes, I didn't believe that it would be a murder conviction."

Jean Griffith declared that she was "pleased" with the jury's verdict. Cedric Sandiford echoed that sentiment.

The verdict came as the residents of Howard Beach were preparing to celebrate Christmas. Their homes had always been over-draped with lavish Christmas decorations and an excessive number of lights, but Christmas 1987 was more subdued than usual. The verdict was denounced by Howard Beach residents, especially by the families and friends of the mobsters. Although they knew well what had happened, most of them expressed the feeling that the sentences were too harsh and that the verdict was a political one.

Residents who were interviewed did nothing to hide their racist views. Immediately after the verdict, neighborhood residents gathered outside the New Park Plaza shop to express their racist views to television reporters. The special prosecutor, referring to the interviews, said, "It was scary." The feeling was conveyed that any Black person on the streets of this community at the time would have been lynched. The general atmosphere in Howard Beach was not unlike that of the old South when lynch mobs terrorized Blacks.

When asked to comment on the verdict, a bartender who had lived all her life in Howard Beach said of the acquittal of Michael Pirone, "At least somebody didn't get a raw deal." The residents, while displaying extreme racist views, expressed dismay that their community had become an international symbol of prejudice and racism. One resident noted that he had just returned from Florida, where he had met a girl from Czechoslovakia who, upon hearing that he was from Howard Beach asked, "Oh, are you a bad person, then?" Another resident said he had received many letters from old Army buddies. They all asked, "What kind of place is this that you live in?"

Even the young children expressed racist views. For example, a 12-year-old girl said of the convictions, "My mother said it just wasn't right." "My parents told me that the man who died wasn't exactly any angel," was the way an 11-year-old girl put it. And the adults in Howard Beach naively expressed

74

dismay that their community had rightfully become a symbol of racism.

The three convicted felons – Kern, Ladone, and Lester – were sentenced separately by Judge Demakos because he wanted to stress that they were being treated as individuals. The first to be sentenced was Jon Lester because he was already serving a prison sentence of one to three years on a gun possession charge at the time of the Howard Beach trial.

Judge Demakos sentenced Jon Lester to a maximum of 10 to 30 years in prison, that is, two 5-to-15-year terms to run consecutively. He informed Lester that he would have to serve a minimum of 10 years before he would be eligible for parole. Lester was denounced by the judge for the "hatred" and "savageness" displayed by his actions. "What kind of individual do I have before me, who, after witnessing a young Black man get crushed by a car, continues his reckless conduct by savagely beating another Black male with a bat?" he asked. "What happened in Howard Beach – and make no mistake about it – it was a racial incident that triggered off this violence," the judge declared, "what should be obvious to everyone here is that racism breeds hatred and hatred breeds racism and it is a vicious circle."

The judge criticized citizens, mainly from Howard Beach, who had written to him urging leniency for Lester, "What disturbs me about all these letters is that there is no remorse." He pointed out that he had received some 1,500 letters that treated the Howard Beach case as a "political and unwarranted conviction of the community of Howard Beach." "This is not a conviction of the community," he said, adding that almost all of the letters were form letters. When Lester's lawyer, Bryan Levinson, asked for leniency for his client, the judge replied that Lester's actions showed "no remorse, no sense of guilt, no shame, no fear," and that leniency was not in order.

As Lester left the courtroom under heavy guard to return to prison, his supporters (relatives, friends and neighbors) burst into applause, and some yelled "murderer" at the special prosecutor. To them, Lester was a hero.

Some two weeks after the sentencing of Lester, the judge sentenced Scott Kern to 6 to 18 years in prison, a sentence consisting of two consecutive 3-to-9-year terms, one for manslaughter, one for assault. Kern must serve at least 6 years before becoming eligible for parole. Of Kern the judge said, "While Lester was the instigator, the one who recruited all the others, the leader, who exhibited the most hate and thirst for violence, this defendant was a follower." But he added that "even though he may have been a follower, he did participate in the reckless chase of Michael Griffith and following his witnessing of Griffith's death, in the brutal beating of Sandiford." When asked to comment on the sentence, Jean Griffith said, "There is no hate in my heart. We're all mothers. In a case like this, no one wins." The judge echoed this sentiment when he said, "I have not been blind to the torment that the parents of these defendants have gone through and are still going through."

The week after Kern was sentenced, Judge Demakos sentenced the third defendant, Jason Ladone, to 5 to 15 years in prison for his part in the racial attack. Ladone must serve at least 5 years before becoming eligible for parole. Agreeing with the defense attorney, Ronald Rubinstein, that the defendant's background and character had been "exemplary before this incident," he said, "Nevertheless, that night Jason Ladone was a violent person who had participated in the reckless death of Griffith and the vicious assault of Sandiford, and this cannot go unpunished." The judge explained that Ladone's "culpability was less than Kern's and definitely less than Lester's."

When the judge announced Ladone's sentence, the father of Scott Kern yelled, "Bunch of crucifiers you are – Pontius Pilate!" Ladone was the only one of the three convicted mobsters to address the court before sentencing. He read a prepared statement that said in part, "I did not go to this party to hurt anyone or to become involved in any kind of racial incident... I would like to take this opportunity to say publicly, I'm sorry, Mrs. Griffith, for your senseless loss. I'm sorry, Mom and Dad, that your lives have been so violently turned around. And, to the court, I would like to say, one young man is dead and another stands before you." He ended by saying, "I hope I get the opportunity and the time to make my life a productive one." When asked to comment on Ladone's statement, Jean Griffith said simply, "I hope he said it from his heart and not from his lips."

With the sentencing of the three defendants, the first phase of the Howard Beach case had ended, but the memories of this attack and of the racist enclave in which it happened remain. Howard Beach is not just an enclave of racism in the city or the country; on the contrary, it merely reflects the racism so endemic in the United States, albeit in exaggerated form. The attack was clearly not an aberration; rather, it was part of the American Way of Life, as Black people know better than most others. Howard Beach residents may be more overt in their racism, but they are not alone. Indeed, the blatant racism of Howard Beach residents was simply one more manifestation of the Reagan/Koch backlash.

The remaining eight defendants were scheduled to be tried at the same time with two separate juries. However, two of them – Harry Buonocore and Salvatore DeSimone – pleaded guilty to misdemeanor riot charges before the trial and were sentenced to five years probation.

Robert Riley pleaded guilty to a charge of assault in exchange for a lesser charge and became a key prosecution witness. He was sentenced to six months in jail.

At the second Howard Beach trial, Thomas Gucciardo and John Seggese were acquitted of all charges. William Bollander, Thomas Farino, and James Povinelli were convicted of misdemeanor riot charges and were later sentenced to three years probation and 200 hours of community service.

. . .

One of the most striking features of the events surrounding the racial attack and its aftermath was the contrast between the behaviors of the victims and the attackers, their families, and friends. In situations of this type, the oppressed always appear to be more humane and decent than the oppressors, and virtually everything about the incidents at Howard Beach demonstrate this point. Compare, for example, the behavior of the mother of the dead man, Jean Griffith, with that of the mother of his attacker, Jean Lester. The only thing they had in common was their first name. Jean Griffith attended the trial daily, always comporting herself with great dignity, even while listening to the gory details of her son's barbaric death. Jean Lester, on the other hand, showed no remorse for her son's bloody crime. Rather, she continued to maintain that he was innocent, and she adopted the line of the defense attorneys that the trial was unfair. For example, after the trial, she made an appearance on a local right-wing radio show and charged that the judge had "basically acted as a prosecutor" and had deliberately "set out" to have her son and the others convicted. Calling the judge "this so-called custodian of justice," she charged that, "He denied to the defense so much and he allowed so much to the prosecution. His latitude to the prosecution was far wider than anything he ever allowed to the defense, in questioning, in direct examination, in cross-examination." She echoed the defense's position that the attack was not racial but an encounter between two groups, and that the victims had been the aggressors.

In contrast, Jean Griffith, who has been widely praised for her deportment, said during the trial, "It seems like sometimes I want to scream. You have to have the strength to deal with it, or you fall apart." Asked how she felt sitting through the trial each day, she replied, "It kind of hurts, thinking about how he died and what he was." When asked if she ever felt moved to approach the families of the attackers, she said simply, "I don't think it's my place to talk to anyone. I'm here to listen. My son is dead. They have their sons."

During the 12 days of jury deliberations, Blacks in New York held several demonstrations and forums protesting racism. Jean Griffith attended these events regularly, always demonstrating great dignity. Her behavior throughout the ordeal was such that she was compared to Winnie Mandela, wife of the then-jailed Black South African leader. Each day during the trial she was accompanied by her surviving son, Christopher, who, in an interview, said he had hoped for a meeting with the families of the attackers and claimed that they should apologize to his mother. "Right now, I'm looking at my mother shaking every day," he said. "They see that. They should come over to her."

Harold Kern, Scott Kern's father, said he felt no desire to approach the Griffith family. He said, "There's no reason for me to do it. It's not the time and place." The senior Kern steadfastly maintained that his son was innocent, saying that his son had told him, "Daddy, I don't know what happened about anybody getting killed."

Not all white persons to become involved in the case expressed the contempt for Blacks that was so prevalent in Howard Beach. When Theresa Fisher, a 29-year-old mother of two who was visiting her sister in Howard Beach the night of the attack, heard screams and saw the 12 white teenagers beating a Black man, she immediately called the police emergency number to report what she had seen. Later she got into her car and drove around trying to locate the victims. She yelled, "Please come, I'm trying to help you. I want to get you out of the neighborhood."

Because of her role in the affair, she became a key prosecution witness at the trial. She was apprehensive about testifying because just three days before her scheduled appearance, a woman who had testified to a grand jury in an unrelated shooting case had been murdered. Because she had called the police about what she had witnessed, she received many telephone threats at home, forcing her to change her telephone number three times. Her sister sold her house and moved from Howard Beach.

During the cross-examination by defense lawyers who used badgering techniques to intimidate her, Fisher broke down and cried on the witness stand. She did not have to become involved in the incident. As she testified, "I did not want to become involved. I did not want to be here. I still don't want to be here. I was subpoenaed to be here." And she did not have to search the neighborhood for Cedric Sandiford, but her sense of decency dictated that she become involved. In this way,

Theresa Fisher demonstrated more humanity than any other white who participated in incidents in Howard Beach that night. The reward for her decency, rather than praise, was that Howard Beach bigots made her life miserable.

In like manner, Cedric Sandiford, who was initially treated more like a criminal than a victim, demonstrated great dignity and decency. While he stood bloodied, looking at the mutilated body of his stepson, the police questioned him about an unrelated robbery. Stephen Murphy, perhaps the most devious of the defense lawyers, cross-examined Sandiford in his customary fashion, hoping to make the witness lose his composure, but Sandiford proved much too decent and determined for justice to let Murphy's obnoxious questioning break him. Sandiford was clearly angry, and he permitted his honest anger to show. He revealed inner qualities – strength, nobility, and truthfulness – so lacking among the white participants, their families, and friends. Upon the completion of the trial, he thanked the special prosecutor and the jurors. The dignity of Cedric Sandiford no doubt played a key role in the convictions, and it demonstrated to all that he was a man of unusual qualities.

In contrast to Fisher and Sandiford, there were the racist comments and behavior of several other white persons not directly involved in the attack. Two young women college students were interviewed about the case. "If I got killed in Harlem, you wouldn't hear about it," one of them said. "It [the Howard Beach attack] wasn't racial. First of all, they had no business being here. They were looking for trouble." "I think everything got blown out of proportion," said her friend.

Two 16-year-old female friends of the attackers – Claudia Calogero and Laura Castagna – were called by the prosecution to testify at the trial. Both had been passengers with the defendants when they first encountered the Black men. When questioned by the prosecution, both pretended that they could not remember anything that happened during the evening. They could not even remember whether their male companions carried large weapons or not. However, when the defense attorneys questioned them, they suddenly remembered that they had been "very much" frightened that evening because the three Black men had surrounded the car, and one of them, Sandiford, had "stuck his head inside the window."

These two witnesses were reminiscent of the two white prostitutes, Ruby Bates and Victoria Price, in the Scottsboro Boys case in Alabama in the 1930s. These women framed the nine Black teenagers who were sentenced to death for rape. It turned out that the Scottsboro Boys had seen Bates and Price for the first time when they were all arrested. The Blacks, the youngest of whom was 13, became involved in a fight with fellow white vagrants on a moving train. At the next stop, they were pulled off the train by white vigilantes and arrested for the "rape" of Bates and Price. The case lasted for several years, with the final one of the nine leaving prison after 19 years. The point is that, in Howard Beach and Alabama, these white women lied in an attempt to frame Black men. The atmosphere in Howard Beach resembled that of Alabama in the 1930s, with racism being a common feature in both cases.

Residents of Howard Beach and their supporters maintained such hard-core racist attitudes that change is unlikely. The parents pass such attitudes on to their children, and remorse for the murder of a Black man is a notion that cannot penetrate their perverted psyches. This is probably best illustrated by the fundraising campaign to support the appeals of the convictions of the racist mobsters. The following announcement, that appeared in a local news weekly, *The Queens Chronicle,* on March 31, 1988, is so racist, so perverted, and so erroneous that it is reprinted in its entirety here. As Judge Demakos remarked during the sentencing of Jon Lester, "It [the racist attack] could have happened in any other community. The trouble or problem is that the responsible people in each community do not wish to recognize this."

MICHAEL GRIFFITH: HOWARD BEACH

HOWARD BEACH APPEAL FUND
Open Meeting
Tuesday, April 5, 1988, 8:00 P.M.
Our Lady Of Grace School
158-20 101st Street
Howard Beach, N.Y.
We Need Your Support More Than Ever!
Howard Beach Information Sheet

In the late evening of December 19th and early morning hours of December 20, 1986, three black men, one wielding an ice pick, another fueled by cocaine, all with criminal records, began an argument with four teenagers returning home from a party in Howard Beach, Queens. The unfortunate incident which followed this provocation ended with the vehicular death of one of the black men on the Belt Parkway.

Inspired by the irresponsible comments of a number of glib politicians, including Mayor Ed Koch, the news and print media blew the entire incident out of proportion and into an entirely unfair and racist cast. Thus, "Howard Beach" unfairly became a euphemism for racism.

Despite the fact that two of the original provocateurs refused to cooperate with the District Attorney of the County in which the incident occurred, the Governor, Mario Cuomo, appointed a special prosecutor. That prosecutor, Charles J. Hynes, using apparently unlimited funds, joined the politically induced campaign to deprive the defendants of a fair finding of fact and instead, unfairly portrayed the local teenagers involved in the incident as a veritable lynch-mob who chased these men only because the color of their skin was black.

Prosecutor Hynes' case was primarily based upon the testimony of three men: Robert Riley, an alleged participant, and two of the black provocateurs, Timothy Grimes and Cedric Sandiford.

Riley, who agreed to testify in exchange for leniency, was painted as the prosecutor's star witness. Riley's scenario included his admission that despite allegations to the contrary, no one was yelling and no one was chasing Michael Griffith, the deceased, at the time he ran on to the Belt Parkway. Riley also maintained the two of the original instigators had drawn knives. Apparently, however, the jury ignored this testimony. Cedric Sandiford, a 36-year-old illegal alien, convicted criminal and drug abuser, was another of the prosecution's mainstays. Despite the fact that Sandiford offered grossly contradictory statements, the jury apparently overlooked the differences in his stories. Though his description of the youth that he claimed attacked him did not match that of Jon Lester, he was by some legerdemain able to identify Lester in the courtroom.

The case with respect to Sandiford's assault is paticularly suspect. In order to convict the defendants of assault on Sandiford, the prosecutor had to prove that he sustained serious or permanent physical injury. The testimony of the emergency room doctors who treated him, however, indicated that Mr. Sandiford was not seriously injured. Moreover, he was, in fact, released after examination on December 20, 1986 and photographs of him immediately before he went to the hospital reveal no serious injury. Thus, despite the absence of medical evidence, the jury, obviously caught in the racial hysteria fomented by the media, convicted on the charge of Assault 1 as to Sandiford.

Timothy Grimes was the prosecution's third important witness. Grimes, a convicted robber and admittedly an abuser of cocaine, crack and marijuana, has been in trouble with the law since 1980. His obvious disregard for law and authority was evident when, on the witness stand, he shouted obscenities to the entire courtroom. His equally vile physical gestures confirmed the potentially violent reaction of this individual to any type of confrontation. Is it any wonder that the night of December 19th and 20th ended in tragedy? By his own admission at trial, Grimes stated that he pulled a knife and advanced toward the boys. He further conceded that he committed perjury when he denied this in the Grand Jury.

Defendants contend that the trial judge, Thomas Demakos, committed several errors which denied these teenagers simple due process of law. Some of these errors involved requiring the defense, without precedent, to give neutral reasons for the exercise of peremptory challenges. Another error centers around the judge's improper, continuous and unfair interjection into the trial as a second prosecutor. Other errors abound through this 8,000-page record. One interesting issue on appeal will revolve around the judge's failure to declare a mistrial based on the allegation that the jury forewoman had taken notes and was attempting to sell her story through an intermediary.

If one ever had any doubt about the trial judge's unfairness, that doubt was dispelled by the draconian sentences that he meted out. One can only assume that he abandoned even a pretense of independent judicial action because of the pressure of the scores of outside agitators.

The defendants contend that the evidence and lack of evidence demonstrated many reasons to doubt, yet, Jon Lester, Jason Ladone and Scott Kern were convicted on Assault I and Manslaughter II. Undoubtedly and as any informed observer must conclude, these boys were used as scapegoats. The guilty verdict in this case was mandated not by the evidence, but rather, by the media, politicians and outside agitators long before the trial began.

It is now up to us to ensure that our voices are heard. We cannot stand by and allow this injustice to continue. To remain silent is to place all of our rights in jeopardy.

A special fund has been established to aid the families involved to help defray the enormous legal expenses involved in seeking an appeal. We urge you to pledge your support and show your compassion so these convictions can be overturned and this vast injustice corrected.

HOWARD BEACH APPEAL FUND
P.O. BOX 335
STATION B
HOWARD BEACH, NEW YORK 11414

*Your donation is not tax-deductible.

MICHAEL GRIFFITH: HOWARD BEACH

The verdict in the Howard Beach case did not help Blacks, especially males, feel any safer on the streets of New York or any other city in the country. Most Blacks know how much they are hated by most whites, and their frustrations are not likely to be eased by the verdict. Even after the trial, but before the verdict, defense attorney Ronald Rubinstein told a reporter that if the defendants were to be found guilty of murder or manslaughter, "What it means is four White people can't get justice."

Ironically, Jon Lester, clearly the most vicious and racist of the mobsters, had dated Ernestine Washington, a Black student, for several months just before the attack. She denied that he was a racist, saying that "he treated me better than all my other boyfriends, even my Black boyfriends." This indicates more than anything else the twisted mind of the young thug who aspires to become a member of organized crime. Perhaps he will practice his ambition from behind bars during the next few years.

E P I L O G U E

According to a report in the *New York Times*, Timothy Grimes had a troubled life before he became a victim of the racist violence that brought Howard Beach to international attention, and the trouble intensified with the attack and trial. According to his mother, Martha Grimes, he had been diagnosed of serious lead poisoning at the age of two. This disease, which can damage the brain and the nervous system, resulted from his eating paint chips. Consequently, he was unable to finish the seventh grade. His mother said he had been very slow in school.

Before the Howard Beach attack, Timothy Grimes had a history of drug use, and he had served 18 months in jail for a robbery in Brooklyn where, along with three other youths, he was convicted of the crime. Shortly after the Howard Beach attack, he was charged with stabbing the woman with whom he lived.

Following the attack in Howard Beach, he was examined by a psychiatrist who testified at the trial that Grimes was "depressed and hyper-vigilant" as a result of post-traumatic stress syndrome that he suffered from the attack. The doctor explained that Grimes was experiencing psychotic episodes in which he imagined that he was being chased by gangs of people. His mother reported that after the Howard Beach attack, Grimes began having nightmares. Around this time, he decided to leave Brooklyn and move to a small Virginia town to live with his brother in an effort to "straighten out his life."

Timothy Grimes took $5,000 with him to Virginia, and shortly after his arrival, he made a loan of $1,200 to his brother. The brother agreed to repay the loan in installments. But according to law enforcement officials, after an argument, Grimes shot his brother with a shotgun he had purchased for hunting. At the trial, Grimes admitted that he was angry because his brother had threatened him, but insisted that he had not meant to hit his brother when he fired the rifle.

His mother said, "My baby is sick. They should have mercy on him." The 61-year-old Martha Grimes and her husband Charles, an unemployed truck driver, had left their home in New York for a short vacation in Virginia but decided to remain there indefinitely after the shooting.

MICHAEL GRIFFITH: HOWARD BEACH

On April 6, 1989, Timothy Grimes was sentenced to 16 years in prison for injuring his brother. The judge allowed that Grimes' terrifying experience in Howard Beach was a mitigating factor in his sentence.

Life's nightmare continues for Timothy Grimes.

4

JOSEPH CHRISTOPHER: MASS MURDERER

OVERVIEW

Four Black men were stabbed to death on the streets of mid-town Manhattan during an 8-hour period on the afternoon and evening of December 22, 1980. All the stabbings took place between 3:30pm and 11:50pm in an area bounded by 33rd and 49th streets, Madison and Seventh avenues. In each case, the attacker thrust a knife once into the victim's chest through heavy clothing, then walked away. The suspect was described as a white male in his early thirties or forties, about five feet, six inches tall, weighing about 140 pounds.

THE ACCOUNT

The police reported the following incidents that occurred in Manhattan: at 3:30pm, Luis Rodriguez, a 19-year-old messenger, was stabbed on Madison Avenue between 40th and 41st streets; at 6:47pm, Antoine Davis, 30, was stabbed at 37th Street near 7th Avenue; Richard Renner, a man in his twenties, was assaulted on 49th Street between Broadway and 7th Avenue at 10:40pm; and at 11:55pm, an unidentified man believed to be in his thirties was found stabbed outside Pennsylvania Station and Madison Square Garden on 33rd Street between 7th and 8th avenues.

In addition, the police reported that 32-year-old Ivan Frazer claimed he had been attacked by a white man at 1:25pm the same day at an IND subway station at 53rd Street and 3rd Avenue. Frazer said he raised his hand to fend off a knife and received cuts to his hand. John Adams, 25, was reported to have been stabbed by a white man on the IRT 14th Street subway platform at 11:30am on the same day. Stuckey Anderson, a 38-year-old Bronx man, told police that a white man came after him with a knife, but he pushed the man down the subway steps.

Four days after undergoing a four-hour operation for a stab wound in the heart, John Adams described the incident for police: "I was coming out of the train, the downtown number 2, at 14th Street. When I got off the subway there was a man walking in front of me. If he was on the train, I didn't notice him. As I was going toward the stairs he suddenly turned around and stabbed me. I thought he punched me. I didn't realize I was stabbed until I got upstairs and felt the blood."

Detectives in New York City called detectives in Buffalo for information about four Black males, including a 14-year-old, who were killed there during a three-day period in September 1980. They suspected that the recent New York City stabbings had been committed by the same person. In April 1981, New York City detectives flew to Fort Benning, Georgia, to inquire about a 25-year-old white Army private who was a possible suspect in the murders of the four Buffalo men and four more men from Rochester.

Private Joseph Christopher joined the Army on November 13, shortly after six of the eight killings in Buffalo and Rochester, and was on leave from December 19 to January 4 when the other two upstate killings and the four in New York City occurred. Shortly after his enlistment, he was hospitalized in a Fort Benning hospital for a self-inflicted razor wound. The nature of his wound was not disclosed in detail; the hospital report noted simply that it had been caused by a razor blade and affected the groin area. Christopher became an official suspect in the New York slayings when Army nurses reported that while being treated, he had bragged to them about killing Black men in New York City and Buffalo. In addition, Christopher was transferred from the hospital to the Fort Benning stockade after he stabbed a 21-year-old Black soldier on January 13, 1981.

Christopher was born in Buffalo on July 26, 1955. His father was the son of Italian immigrants and worked for the Buffalo sanitation department until his death in 1975. His mother was a registered nurse. Christopher had three sisters. He had never been to New York City before the killings. Records indicate that he arrived in New York City on December 20 and returned to Buffalo either December 24 or 25.

A search of Christopher's home in Buffalo and a family hunting cabin in Ellington, New York, some 40 miles southwest, turned up several items of interest: six knives, nine boxes of .22-caliber ammunition, ten .22-caliber bullet casings, two sawed-off gun stocks, a .22-caliber barrel, a black Navy watch cap and a green Army-style rain jacket that was stained with blood. A subsequent test of the jacket showed that it contained human blood stains.

The trail of violence has been detailed as follows: the 12 homicides in the three cities (Buffalo, Rochester, and New York) began in Buffalo on September 22, 1980, when four Black men were shot in the head by a gunman. On October 8 and 9, two Black men were slain, and their hearts were cut out. On December 22, six men were stabbed in mid-town Manhattan, four of them fatally. A Buffalo man was stabbed to death on December 29, and a Black man in Rochester was fatally stabbed the next day. Another Black man barely survived a stab wound to the heart in Buffalo on December 31. And in Fort Benning, Georgia, on January 13, 1981, a Black soldier was stabbed, for which Christopher was spending time in the stockade.

The District Attorney in Buffalo presented the case to a grand jury, and an indictment was issued for three of the seven deaths in the Buffalo area, based largely on physical evidence seized at the Christopher family's hunting cabin. Two nurses from Fort Benning testified before the grand jury that Christopher had told them that he had killed Black men in New York City in December 1980. When an Army medical officer asked him why he had committed the alleged crimes, he answered simply, "I had to," the same reply he had given when the nurses posed the same question.

Christopher was turned over to police in Georgia, but he refused to waive his right to extradition as the District Attorney in Buffalo had requested. He insisted on a formal extradition hearing. Meanwhile, the District Attorney back in Buffalo announced on May 1, 1981, that he had recovered spent .22-caliber shells at Christopher's home and that they matched those found at the scene of four of the shootings. The gun, a sawed-off rifle, had apparently been fired at close range. Also found was a double-edged sheath knife. Police said the knife was similar to the one that had been used in the stabbings.

The Buffalo District Attorney requested formally that Christopher be extradited to Buffalo, and the governor of Georgia signed the request for Christopher's extradition on May 2, 1981. The extradition took place on May 8. Among his possessions, detectives found a bus ticket for a December 19 trip from Fort Benning to New York City with arrival scheduled for December 20. Two days later, four Black men were stabbed to death in New York City.

Back in Buffalo, Christopher pleaded not guilty to the murders that had taken place there. He asked to conduct his own defense at his trial. The judge ordered him held without bail and demanded that he undergo psychiatric examinations. When Christopher appeared in a line-up, he was recognized by persons who had witnessed his crimes, both in Buffalo and in

New York City. Two legal aid lawyers were appointed by the court to assist him in his defense.

People who had known Christopher in Buffalo expressed surprise that he had been charged in the racially motivated murders. Black and white friends of the accused said that he had not shown any racial animosity in the past. A Black man who had worked with him said that the only racial remark he had made was that he had been "ripped off" by some Blacks when he was a boy but that "He didn't seem to have any strong feelings about race." Indeed, he frequently socialized with Blacks.

The Manhattan District Attorney presented his case to a grand jury. The grand jury indicted Christopher for one of the New York City murders. Officials of USAir, a commercial airline, refused to fly Christopher from Buffalo to New York City. They feared bombs or other attacks on the airplane. They cited their policy of not transporting "people who are known to be dangerous." A charter airline was hired for the trip.

In New York, as in Buffalo, Christopher pleaded not guilty to the charge of murder at his arraignment in Manhattan State Supreme Court. He was returned to the Erie County Jail in Buffalo to await trial.

The Buffalo trial commenced on October 1981. Disregarding advice from his court-appointed legal counsel, Christopher waived his right to be tried by a jury, opting for a trial by the judge (bench trial). When asked about his decision, he told the judge, "I figure you're an educated man. You know the law. You're a judge." His trial was delayed when the judge ordered him to undergo psychiatric tests to determine if he knew what he was doing when he waived a jury trial. This caused a further delay.

On December 16, 1981, a state Supreme Court justice in Buffalo ruled that Christopher was not mentally competent to stand trial. He ordered that the accused be placed in a mental institution. Under the law his case could be reviewed within one year to determine if he had regained his fitness to stand trial. During the hearing, two psychiatrists for the prosecution argued that he was fit to stand trial, while two for the defense said he was not. This was just another case in which "hired gun" psychiatrists said what they were paid to say. They are sometimes called "pimp" psychiatrists, and their testimonies are usually exercises in futility.

In New York City, the Manhattan District Attorney announced that he would continue to press his case against Christopher. However, in February, Christopher was diagnosed unfit for trial in New York City. He was sent to the Mid-Hudson State Psychiatric Center in Beacon, New York. On February 17, 1982, the director of the hospital reported that Christopher had been found mentally competent to stand trial. Christopher had himself requested that he be released from the hospital. On March 23, he was found fit to stand trial in Buffalo, and a trial date was set.

The Buffalo trial finally commenced on April 12, 1982. Christopher's mother, a sister, and an aunt were in attendance. The prosecution rested its case on April 21, and the defense rested its case after two days of testimony. Altogether, the prosecution presented 38 witnesses. A nurse from Fort Benning (Georgia) testified that Christopher had told her about the killings when she asked him if he had read about them in the newspaper. He told her that something had just come over him and that it was something he had to do.

Christopher was found guilty of three killings. He showed no emotion as the verdict was read. The Manhattan District Attorney announced that he would be brought to New York City for trial shortly after the sentencing in Buffalo.

Christopher received a sentence of 60 years to life in prison for the murders of Glenn Dunn, 14, who had been fatally shot in a car parked in the lot of a supermarket on September 22; Harold Green, 32, who was killed on September 23 while eating lunch in his car in Cheektowaga, a Buffalo suburb; and Emanuel Thomas, 32, who was killed while walking down a street in Buffalo. The sentence requires that Christopher serve 60 years before becoming eligible for parole.

Nearly five years after the first murders in Buffalo, the New York Court of Appeals ruled that the trial judge in Buffalo had erred in not calling for the psychiatric testimony requested by the defense. By a vote of 4-2, the court ruled that Christopher should have a hearing on his psychological fitness to stand trial.

Christopher was hospitalized at the Central New York Psychological Center in Marcy, New York, near Utica. He was transferred there for treatment in May from the state prison in Auburn. While incarcerated there, he was tried in New York

City for the murder of one man and the attempted murder of another. He was found guilty of these charges on October 23, 1985. He was still facing trial for the death of a Black man in Niagara Falls, New York, in September 1980. Meanwhile, back in Buffalo, he was re-tried and convicted of murder and attempted murder. He was sentenced to the maximum term: 33-and-a-half years in prison.

5

WILLIAM TURKS: GRAVESEND

OVERVIEW

One Black man was killed and two others injured when their car stalled on a street in the Gravesend section of Brooklyn in the early hours of June 22, 1982. A mob of white youths attacked the victims without provocation as they were going home from their jobs as maintenance workers for the New York City Transit Authority.

Close to midnight, Willie Turks, 34, Dennis Dixon, 30, and Donald Cooper, 30, decided to stop at the Avenue X Bagels shop on 357 Avenue X for a snack. As they approached the shop, they were accosted by three white youths yelling threats and racial slurs. Dennis Dixon, a Brooklyn native and one of the two survivors, said, "They came at us, yelling 'Niggers get out of here.'"

When the victims attempted to drive away, their car stalled. When Dixon, the driver, got out to check the motor, one of the youths ran up to him and hit him on the side of the head with a beer bottle. The three youths were suddenly joined by 15 or 20 others who surounded the car and smashed windows with everything from beer bottles and cans to a long iron rod. Dixon and Cooper, of Far Rockaway, Queens, managed to break loose and run, going in opposite directions. But William Turks, also from Far Rockaway, was caught and fatally beaten by the mob on Avenue X near East 1st street.

In describing what they called the "racially motivated" attack, the police said that four or five youths wrenched Turks from the car and dragged him across Avenue X, where he was beaten and kicked. The mob then left their victim bleeding and unconscious, lying on a street corner below an apartment building. Turks, who suffered massive skull and brain injuries, died three hours later at Coney Island Hospital.

According to police officers, members of the community responded quickly to the plight of the victim, with seven calls to the emergency 911 number and more to the precinct house. The commander of Brooklyn detectives said that the case would be solved without delay. "We don't want any hostilities lingering in the area," they said.

Many of Gravesend's community leaders and residents complained that Avenue X had long been a trouble spot, a hangout for crowds of local young people. One merchant remarked that youth liked to drink beer there until the early hours of the morning.

Overall, Gravesend was described by residents as an area with few racial problems. However, the police said there had been other incidents with racial overtones.

(1) An off-duty Black housing authority policeman had been attacked by a group of whites on the same section of Avenue X on May 3, 1981, slightly more than one year before the attack on Turks, Cooper, and Dennis. Robert Fountain had finished his 4:00p.m.-midnight shift at the Coney Island housing project. He stopped at the Avenue X Bagels Shop because he was hungry and wanted to pick up something to eat before going home. As he emerged from the coffee shop something smashed into the side of his head. He fell, and a group of young white toughs began kicking and jumping on him. One yelled, "Kill the nigger." Fountain then said, "I'm a police officer." The officer drew his revolver from an ankle holster, but someone kicked the revolver as it discharged, and the bullet struck Fountain in the ankle. The youths fled, and Fountain was treated for wounds to the ankle and other injuries. While watching news about Turks' murder on television, Fountain recognized the person primarily responsible for Turks' death as the same person who had led the attack on him. Despite the fact that Fountain identified the perpetrator, no one was ever arrested in this case.

(2) In April 1982, a 30-year-old Black man, Frank Tyrrell, was attacked while leaving the same bagel shop at 1:30am. He

had stopped there on his way home to Queens. After leaving the shop, he was hit on the back of his head with such force that he remained in a coma for several days. Like the Fountain case, no one was ever arrested.

(3) In May 1982, the police were called to break up a melee that erupted between Black and white youths at James Madison High School near Kings Highway and 16th Street.

When asked why nothing had been done in these recent incidents, Captain Joseph DeMartini, Commander of the 61st precinct, said, "There is a youthful population in that part of Brooklyn and you tend to have kids on corners." He further noted that they were primarily neighborhood youths. "The large majority of these youths are good decent people and are appalled by what happened. There are a lot of good kids out there who are going to develop into outstanding adults." DeMartini called Gravesend a typical community. "We are aware of all these incidents. But to say a Black gets assaulted and to say it's racial, I don't know. You have to make that distinction between intentional acts as compared to random assault," he said.

But would the captain have been so philosophical if these attacks had been caused by Black or Hispanic youths? There appears to be a tendency to explain away racial attacks when committed by whites against Blacks. Also, might Turks still be alive today had the other incidents been investigated, arrests made, and the perpetrators punished? The refusal to make arrests might have given the thugs the message that one is not convicted for crimes against Blacks, no matter how serious. Indeed, the same person was identified as the major attacker in at least two of these incidents.

Contrary to the prevalent cavalier attitude, not all people explained away these attacks. Alvin Blau, the owner of a driving school on Avenue X close to where the assault took place, said, "I've seen this kind of thing here. Racial remarks have been addressed to me when I'm in a car with a Black student."

On the other hand, the mother of one of the attackers accused Blacks who had recently moved to nearby Coney Island of committing criminal acts in her neighborhood. "There are lots of incidents happening with the colored," she said. "They raped a girl in the laundry room. Another woman was tied up in her apartment. This is what riled up these boys," she said, trying to justify the killing of William Turks.

Gravesend is described as a community of neat, prosperous homes; the annual median income was $23,000 at the time of the attack. The community was named by Lady Deborah Moody in 1643, for the hometown she left in England in search of greater religious freedom. Gravesend is predominantly Italian and Jewish, but a handful of Blacks have settled there in recent years. Indeed, as if to prove the existence of racial harmony in that community, white residents pointed to the four Black families who lived in the apartment house where the leader of the mob lived. Another Black family lived next door.

THE VICTIMS
William Turks was separated from his wife; they had a 10-year-old daughter. Dennis Dixon, one of the two who survived

the attack, was a vegetarian who jogged and practiced yoga. When each of his three children were born, Dixon assisted in the delivery at home. During the attack, he was struck on the head with a bottle, which caused him to suffer headaches, violent nightmares, and a loss of hearing. Dixon reported that when he first contacted the police, they did not go immediately to the aid of Turks. Moreover, he claimed that when his wound was treated, it had been closed with the glass left inside. The injury caused him to be out of work for three months, during which time he received no sick pay or other benefits. His ambition had been to open a welding business, but the $1,700 that he had saved toward this project was required for his living expenses while he was recuperating.

THE TRIAL

The day after the attack on Turks, Dennis and Cooper, two teenagers were arrested in the fatal beating. Gino Bova, an 18-year-old high school student, was arrested in the Manhattan office of his lawyer, Paul Callan. Later that same morning, police arrested Paul Moromonda at his home. Both lived in Gravesend.

On the day of the attack, the three transit workers were making their second visit to the Avenue X Bagel Shop. Dennis Dixon recalled that when they first entered the shop, a number of young men were hanging around, and "one of the guys outside the store was calling us names." He said that on the next visit the same taunter was there and began to shout at them again. He identified Gino Bova as the person responsible, just as Robert Fountain had identified him as his assailant in the 1981 attack.

Both Bova and Moromonda were charged with second-degree murder in criminal court in Brooklyn and were held without bail. Both were put into protective custody at the request of their lawyers, who cited the youth of the defendants and the circumstances of the case as reasons for this request.

The police reported that they had witnesses who had "named names" in the case and that "some of the witnesses had some involvement in the case." Based on this information, they arrested 19-year-old Anthony Miccio. He was charged with two felonies: riot in the first degree and assault in the first degree. Miccio was tried, convicted, and received a 3-to-9-year sentence in prison.

On June 28, 1982, two more suspects in the mob assault were arrested, bringing the total to five. Those newly arrested were Anthony Burmedez, 26, and Danny Stola, 20. Both were charged with first-degree assault and inciting a riot.

Meanwhile, Blacks in New York demonstrated to protest the slaying of Willie Turks. Hundreds marched in front of the Avenue X Bagel Shop. One organizer of the demonstration announced, "I am officially declaring this area open to Black people." The crowd chanted, "Gino, Gino, you can't hide – we charge you with genocide."

Gino Bova's trial commenced on March 1, 1983. The jury that heard his trial consisted of 11 whites and one Hispanic, but no Blacks – a situation created by defense lawyers, who challenged from the jury pool all Black persons.

One of the initial witnesses from Gravesend, a 19-year-old, referred to Blacks as "the colored," a description that denotes so well the prejudice of Bova's community.

Dennis Dixon testified that while bleeding and lying unconscious, one member of the mob shouted, "Hit that nigger." Dennis quoted Bova as saying, "What are you niggers doing in this area?" and "Niggers, get out of here."

Gino Bova was convicted of second-degree manslaughter in Turks' death. He was also convicted of first-degree assault, first-degree riot, and discrimination. The jury in the case deliberated for two days. Bova faced a maximum sentence of 5 to 15 years in prison. The lawyer for Paul Moromonda asked that his client's trial be delayed because of the publicity accompanying the Bova trial.

Bova was sentenced on March 31, 1983, nearly one year after he committed the brutal murder. Judge Sybil Hart Kooper told the packed courtroom, "There was a lynch mob on Avenue X that night. The only thing missing was a rope and a tree." She then sentenced Bova to the maximum possible term – 5 to 15 years. Bova must serve at least five years before being considered for parole.

The second attacker, Paul Moromonda, went on trial in July 1983, charged with second-degree murder. He was also charged with assault, riot, and illegal discrimination. The prosecutor charged that Moromonda had acted "with depraved indifference to human life." The jury of eight whites, one Black, and three Hispanics cleared him of the murder and felony charges but convicted him of four misdemeanors: third-degree assault, second-degree riot, and two counts of discrimination. The jury trial lasted one week, and the jury deliberated one day. For his actions, despite his mother's justification of the attack, Moromonda received two one-year terms.

The District Attorney dropped all charges against Daniel Stola when a witness recanted her testimony. She had placed Stola at the scene of the beating but later changed her testimony. Paul Moromonda was released from prison on March 14, 1984, after serving seven months. He was given time off for good behavior.

In the meantime, the last of the six white youths sought in the case surrendered to police on June 12, 1984. Joseph Powell, 29, was accompanied by his grandfather, Giro Laguori. Powell had been indicted by a grand jury, charged with second-degree murder, assault, riot, and discrimination. Five others were indicted and three (Bova, Moromonda, and Micco) were convicted on various charges. Anthony Bermudez and Daniel Stola were also indicted. Burmedez was fatally shot on January 1, 1983, before trial, and charges against Stolla were dropped.

Joseph Powell, 28, who had been a fugitive in the case, pleaded guilty to an assault charge on April 15, 1985. Detectives had traced him to Connecticut, Florida, New Jersey, and Pennsylvania. He accepted a plea bargain, part of which stipulated that the judge sentence him to from 3 to 9 years in prison. The assault charge carries a maximum penalty of 5 to 15 years. At his sentencing, Powell said to the 66-year-old

mother of Willie Turks, "I'm truly sorry Mr. Turks was killed."
The judge noted that Powell did not admit his role in the assault.

This case had all the earmarks of similar trials, with one final irony: Gino Bova's lawyer requested that his client be spared a prison sentence because, as he put it, he would be in grave danger in prison, where Blacks are in such large numbers. In other words, he was afraid that his client would become a victim of the very crime for which he was convicted. The judge ignored this perverted request.

6

MICHAEL STEWART:
ARTIST AND MODEL

OVERVIEW

"As Stewart lay helpless, face down on the sidewalk, with his hands still cuffed behind his back, he was repeatedly kicked by transit officers. As the beating continued, Stewart's screams became less loud and intense, until he fell silent." This was how the first indictment against transit police officers accused in the death of Michael Stewart read.

The death of Michael Stewart, a 25-year-old artist and model, in the early morning hours of September 15, 1983, outraged New York's Black community and others concerned with racial justice. Stewart's death was one of the most highly publicized incidents of violence against Black people, either by the police or civilians, in recent years.

THE ACCOUNT

According to transit authority police officers, sometime around 3:30am on September 15, a transit authority policeman noticed Stewart on the IND subway platform at 1st Avenue and 14th Street scrawling graffiti on the wall. When approached, he reportedly became violent and struggled with the officer, who then radioed for assistance. Altogether, 11 officers (all of them white) arrived and assisted in the arrest. Stewart was then put into a police van and was transported to Bellevue Hospital for psychiatric observation. He arrived at the hospital comatose, in handcuffs, and his legs were bound with tape. Stewart never regained consciousness; he died 13 days later on September 28.

The accounts of the district attorney and of persons who observed the incident differed sharply from that of the police. The district attorney maintained that transit police officers used billy clubs and night sticks, fatally wounding Stewart as he lay helpless and handcuffed on the sidewalk. It was maintained that Stewart was hog-tied by two transit police officers and "forcibly thrown or tossed" into a van after the beating. "His body was seen by some to fly through the air before it landed in the van's storage compartment," according to the initial indictment. "Transit officers struck Stewart's prone and defenseless body with their billy clubs or night sticks. One witness even saw Stewart being choked with a nightstick."

The Medical Examiner's autopsy report played a crucial role in the Stewart case. The Medical Examiner's report was issued by Dr. Elliot Gross, Chief Medical Examiner, on September 29, 1983. The report claimed that Stewart's injuries were not linked to his death. Gross maintained that while Stewart was in police custody, he suffered a heart attack and lapsed into a coma; two days later, he was dead from heart failure. "There is no evidence of physical injury resulting in or contributing to death," Gross said. Regarding the bruises on his wrist, Gross said, "The bruises could have been caused by a number of things, including a beating or a fall," but the wounds "were consistent" with injuries caused by manacles.

But a lawyer retained by the Stewart family disputed Gross' conclusion. Attorney Louis Clayton Jones maintained that the autopsy, which was witnessed for the family by Dr. John Grauerholz, Assistant Medical Examiner of Passaic County, New Jersey, showed that Stewart's death had been caused by strangulation. According to Dr. Grauerholz, pinpoint bleeding, known as a petechial hemorrhage, had been seen in the eyes during the autopsy. According to pathologists, such hemorrhages are a standard sign of strangulation. Because the blood flow from the head is cut off, blood backs up, causing the vessels in the eyes to burst.

The Stewart family asked the Mayor to replace Dr. Gross, claiming that not only was the report filled with contradictions, but apparently Gross had removed the eyes of the young artist after the autopsy. The family maintained that the eyes had been removed after Dr. Grauerholz reported that signs of hemorrhaging in the eyes raised the possibility that Stewart had been strangled by the transit police. But lawyers for the Medical Examiner's office said that Gross did not need family permission to remove body parts during an autopsy.

An investigation by the *New York Times* found that the handling of the Stewart autopsy was an extraordinary mixture of contradictions, and in the opinions of many people, there was blatant deception. "Dr. Gross has lied," said Dr. Robert Wolf, one of the Stewart family doctors and a professor of medicine at Mount Sinai Medical Center. "He has couched the lie in language that is so obviously absurd that, even without any medical education, people should be able to deduce that he lied." Dr. Wolf's assertion was supported by pathologists in the Medical Examiner's office as well as other doctors engaged by the Stewart family.

When he went to Bellevue Hospital to examine Stewart's body, Dr. Wolf said, "I removed the sheets and it was obvious that he had incurred trauma to all major portions of his body, without exception. I determined that the most likely source of the wounds was a beating."

The police then made the following accusations: Stewart resisted arrest because he was on drugs; Stewart became violent after his arrest and had to be restrained; and cocaine was found on Stewart. They were later forced to recant this last assertion.

More details about the autopsy procedure were reported to the public. It was learned that two transit police detectives had been permitted to join Dr. Gross and Dr. Grauerholz in the autopsy room. The procedure began at 1:30pm and lasted for more than six hours. Gross took hundreds of photographs. At about 7:45pm, he completed the autopsy and returned to his office. Then he met privately with a transit authority detective.

Several minutes later, Gross held a news conference and issued a written statement of his preliminary findings. It read: "The cause of death is cardiac arrest pending further study. The autopsy disclosed findings consistent with the hospital course of prolonged coma, followed by a cardiac arrest, and there was no evidence of physical injury resulting or contributing to death."

The medical stenographer, Siegfried Oppenheim, who took the dictation from Dr. Gross, said, "I was horrified. Gross has completely disregarded the history of the case and the photographs. Where was the mention of the bruises in the cause of death? Where was the mention of the fact that he died in police custody? You're supposed to put all of that in the autopsy report." Oppenheim, who said he has witnessed 10,000 autopsies over a period of 40 years, resigned from his post. "I want nothing to do with that place," he stated.

According to Dr. Wolf, the autopsy revealed 60 hemor-rhages all over the body. Yet, in describing the cause of death, the preliminary autopsy report recorded only, "Cardiac arrest with survival for 13 days. Broncho-pneumonia: pending further study." Several doctors testified that they were appalled by that finding. "He said that the cause of death was cardiac arrest, yet he describes no intrinsic cardiac disease whatso-ever," said Dr. Wolf. "What Dr. Gross was really saying was that Stewart died because his heat stopped beating, but that doesn't mean anything." Dr. Wolf called Gross' statement that physical injury had not caused the death "an outrageous statement – it's called a 'blatant lie.' "

Furthermore, the Stewart family maintained that Dr. Gross agreed to notify their doctors before performing any operations. The doctors should have been allowed to observe all procedures. But on September 30, the day after the autopsy, Dr. Gross returned to the autopsy room alone and removed Stewart's eyes.

According to Dr. Grauerholz, Dr. Gross placed the eyes in a container of formalin, a solution that preserves tissue but tends to wash out any trace of blood. "It bleaches out the red cells," he said.

Dr. Gross maintained in court documents that the eyes were removed only after attempts were made to reach Dr. Grauerholz by telephone. But Dr. Grauerholz disputed that. He said that his telephone had an automatic answering machine and that no messages from Dr. Gross or any other city official were left on it. Dr. Grauerholz said that he was informed that the eyes had been removed several days after the fact, when Dr. Gross telephoned to discuss other tissue samples.

Dr. Wolf declared that there was no medically sound reason for Dr. Gross' action. "The removal of the eyes was superfluous. At minimum it was irrelevant. At maximum it may be seen as illegal." The Stewart family filed a civil law suit against Gross, seeking damages for his handling of the case and charging that the removal of the eyes was an attempt to obstruct justice by destroying the evidence of hemorrhaging.

On December 2, several weeks after the initial autopsy, Dr. Gross called a news conference to announce his final conclusions about the death. In a complete departure from prior statements, the Medical Examiner's report showed that Stewart had died from a "physical injury to the spinal cord in the upper neck." Under questioning, he refused to say what caused the injury. The cause of death was given as "Upper Cervical Transverse with survival for 13 days. Ischemic cerebral necrosis, Broncho-pneumonia. Collapsed while in police custody on September 15, 1983." In other words, Stewart died of a spinal cord injury resulting from the absence of oxygen after his heart stopped.

Attorney Jones said that Dr. Gross had blamed the death on spinal injuries because it might fit with the police report that Stewart hurt himself in a chase during the arrest.

The new finding was disputed by two of the Stewart family pathologists, Drs. Grauerholz and Wolf. Stewart died, they said, after having been choked, possibly with a night stick; the choking cut off the supply of oxygenated blood to the brain. "It is simple," Dr. Grauerholz said. "Without oxygen in his brain, Stewart went into cardiac arrest. Since his heart was not beating, he stopped sending blood up north. When he was finally resuscitated, enough damage had already been done to the brain that he didn't wake up again." He said that if Dr. Gross was right about the spinal injuries, the spine would have been severely fractured or dislocated. "But there wasn't anything like that." Moreover, he said that Dr. Gross' findings would require hemorrhages near the spine to date back to the altercation with the police – the bleeding should have been at least 13 days old. But tissue slides showed that the bleeding was recent, which indicated that it had been a *result* of death, not its cause.

The autopsy also had been observed by Dr. Josette Montas, one of Gross' chief deputies. But contrary to custom, her signature did not appear on the autopsy report, which, some doctors said, indicated her disagreement with Dr. Gross.

The Stewart family was annoyed with Gross' refusal to classify the death as a homicide. Without a homicide finding, prosecutors found it difficult to pursue criminal charges. Dr. Wolf charged, "It was homicide. I am clear on this conclusion with a confidence approaching 100 percent. And Dr. Gross tried to cover it up."

Because of the controversy over the autopsy report, District Attorney Robert Morganthau submitted the autopsy to an outside consultant, Dr. William Brownlee, a Black pathologist from Washington, DC. While Dr. Brownlee praised Dr. Gross, he would not say whether he agreed with the findings in the autopsy report. Dr. Brownlee is not board-certified in pathology, and the Stewarts maintained that choosing a Black doctor was "a public relations ploy that is insulting."

. . .

Michael Stewart was a young artist and model who lived with his parents in the Cobble Hill section of Brooklyn. At the

118

time of the tragedy, his mother was a retired school teacher, and his father was an employee with the New York City Transit Authority.

The Michael Stewart case was one of the most troubling and perhaps one of the most blatant of its type in recent history. One wonders why 11 police officers could not restrain one man, who weighed only 135 pounds, without taking his life. The police maintained that Stewart attempted to escape when apprehended, that he fell on the subway steps, that necessary force was used to subdue him, and that he lapsed into a coma en route to Bellevue Hospital. But many troubling questions remained unanswered. What caused the bruises to the face, wrist, and other parts of Stewart's body? Why was the Medical Examiner at first so definite that force had not been used? Why did Gross change his opinion on the cause of death? Why did he telephone both the Mayor's and District Attorney's offices before commencing the autopsy? Why did he constantly confer with transit authority officers during the autopsy?

It is important to note that Michael Stewart's death occurred during the period when the Committee Against Racially Motivated Violence was preparing a paper on cases of police brutality to present to the House Subcommittee on Criminal Justice, which was convening in New York City to hold hearings on police brutality. City officials had maintained that police brutality was neither widespread nor systemic. Members of the Congressional committee had been invited to New York by leaders in the Black community.

It is also important to note that in 1984, transit officers were falsely arresting Black and Hispanic men, including plain-clothes police officers, and charging them with a variety of crimes, usually sexual abuse of white women, when no crimes in fact had occurred. This information became public in November 1987 and was subsequently investigated. Indeed, one plain-clothes Black policeman won a judgement of $400,000 for false arrest.

This shocking series of incidents was uncovered by Thomas Dargan, a lieutenant retired from the transit police internal affairs unit, whose 1984 investigation of the transit police officers concluded that they had made many wrongful arrests and lied about them. The false arrest of a plain-clothes police officer, Ronald Yeadon, in 1984, was challenged by the officer, who filed a federal lawsuit for "malicious prosecution." This lawsuit prompted disclosure of the report on the situation, which had been withheld.

According to Dargan, the author of the original report that had been generated by the Internal Affairs Unit of the police department, the officers had arrested Black and Hispanic men. Listed as complainants were white women, many of whom said they had been unaware they were crime victims until informed by the officers, nor did they realize that they had pressed charges until the court papers came in the mail.

Of those falsely arrested, 18 percent of the defendants were convicted of the crimes charged, 53 percent pleaded guilty to lesser charges, and 30 percent were found not guilty or had their cases dismissed. Dargan sent the report to District Attorney Morganthau but was told that there was not enough evidence to prosecute the officers for perjury. A departmental hearing was proposed, but instructions were given to close the case and file the report.

In one case, the falsely arrested officer sued the transit authority, and his case was settled for $10,000. Another lawsuit ended in a jury award of $400,000 in 1986.

Is it simply a coincidence that the transit officers involved in this scandal were from District Four, the 14th Street Union Square station, the same place where Michael Stewart met his death at the hands of 11 transit officers?

THE TRIAL

On June 1, 1984, three transit authority police officers were arrested in an indictment charging them with manslaughter in the death of Michael Stewart: Henry Boerner, 40, an 18-year veteran; John Kostick, 25, an officer for two years and; Anthony Piscol, 43, a 17-year veteran. Although the Manhattan District Attorney admitted that other officers might have been involved, no others were indicted. He claimed that the three officers were charged with either directly causing the death of Stewart, or, by their inaction, with permitting other officers to assault him. All three were charged with second-degree manslaughter, criminally negligent homicide, and hindering prosecution.

When the indictment was announced, Attorney Jones remarked that he was "astounded" that the officers had not been charged with the more serious crime of murder and that more officers had not been indicted. "If this had been a White boy who had been beaten by 11 Black officers, you would have had murder indictments within two days," he said.

The indictment noted that the three officers "recklessly engaged in conduct which caused the death of Michael Stewart and recklessly tried to perform acts of which they were physically capable, thereby causing the death of Michael J. Stewart." The three were charged with physically assaulting Stewart or watching as other officers assaulted him. The officers were released without bail.

In an editorial appearing after the indictment, the *New York Times* had this to say: "The Stewart case occurred alarmingly soon after the indictment of Peter Marsala, a transit officer accused of assaulting three men in the course of arresting them. He was convicted in April, and at a sentencing hearing last month the judge criticized the transit police for lack of attention to officers with behavior problems."

The union representing transit police officers called for the dismissal of the grand jury indictment against the three officers because the investigation had been tainted by juror Ronald Fields, a French teacher. The juror was alleged to have conducted his own investigation of Stewart's death. It is said that he then gave his findings to other jurors and discussed the case outside of court.

Fields commenced his own investigation when he discovered that Manhattan prosecutors had attempted to block a murder indictment against the three officers in Stewart's death. Fields had also been accused of disseminating photographs he had made at the site of the attack.

Fields' conduct proved sufficient to have a State Supreme Court justice dismiss the indictment against the three officers. The dismissal charged that the conduct of Fields had "permeated the entire presentation of this case." And it charged that Fields had become what amounted to "an unsworn witness against the defendants."

The District Attorney convened another grand jury in the case, and on February 21, 1985, six transit officers were indicted. Three of the officers were charged with criminally negligent homicide, assault, and perjury; three others were charged with perjury. The grand jury heard testimony from 62 witnesses, including pathologists hired by the Stewart family and some 40 witnesses who said they had seen the beating but could not identify the officers.

This time Henry Boerner, John Kostick, and Anthony Piscola were charged with criminally negligent homicide. James Barry, Henry Hassler, and Susan Techky were charged with perjury. When he was arrested, Stewart was in the custody of Boerner, Kostick and Piscola.

In announcing the indictment, the District Attorney stated, "Here you see we have a classic cover-up situation. We had all the police officers who saw no evil, heard no evil. Nobody saw anybody beat up the prisoner." He maintained that it was impossible to say which officers actually participated in the beating. "What this indictment means," he said, "is that when a police officer makes an arrest, he is responsible for the prisoner in his custody. If he beats him up or permits some other officer to beat him, he is going to be held legally responsible."

The District Attorney pointed out that this was the first time that a criminal case based on the omission of an act had been used against a police officer in New York State. This is a well-established but rarely used theory that a police officer has an affirmative duty to protect his or his prisoner from harm and that, if need be, an officer should arrest whomever tries to harm the prisoner, including a fellow officer.

Jury selection commenced on June 10, 1985, when one of the largest jury pools ever assembled for a criminal case in Manhattan was summoned. Some 290 people made up the pool, and special screening procedures were instituted because of the publicity the case had received. The selection of a jury to try the six police officers turned out to be difficult. After two weeks of screening, no jurors had been selected. Many persons were reluctant to serve because the judge informed them that the trial was likely to last for three months.

Finally, on July 17, a jury was selected, consisting of seven men and five women, two of whom were Hispanic; no Blacks were selected. The trial started on July 18, and in their opening statement the defense attorneys announced that they would prove that Stewart's death resulted from drunkenness, that he died of cardiac arrest brought on by drinking huge amounts of alcohol.

The first witnesses were 23 students from the Parsons School of Design. All of the students lived in a dormitory at 31 Union Square West and had heard Michael Stewart screaming after his arrest. The students had witnessed the incident from a window and were therefore unable to identify any of the police officers involved.

The first student to testify was 20-year-old Rebecca Reiss. She described how, from her fifth-floor window, she saw police officers kick and strike Stewart as he screamed for help. "Oh, my God, someone help me, someone help me," Stewart yelled as he was pushed to the ground, she said. She recalled observing the police putting handcuffs on him: "One of the officers was kicking the man, and the other officers were hitting the man." Soon after the beating, she testified, Stewart was "silent." His hands and feet were tied behind his back, and he was "thrown into a van," which then drove off.

Three of Michael Stewart's friends, who worked at the Pyramid Club where Stewart had spent the evening, testified next. All of them said he showed no signs of drunkenness in the hours before his arrest. Tests made at Bellevue Hospital showed his blood alcohol content to be .22 percent, more than twice the .01 standard for intoxication in New York motor vehicle law. The defense had also maintained that there were several "drug-related" items in his clothing, including a half-used marijuana cigarette, a cut-off straw and a mirror used for taking cocaine, and an empty glassine envelope. These witnesses said they had been with Stewart most of the evening of his arrest and that he had not used drugs. Furthermore, medical tests at Bellevue Hospital showed no trace of drugs, other than alcohol, in his body.

Another witness, Robert Rodriguez, a former auxiliary police officer, told the jury that he had witnessed the beating of Stewart on the night of the arrest. Fearing a cover-up, he stated that he went over to where the police were beating Stewart and said, "Listen and listen good. I don't want any cover-up." Rodriguez testified that when the incident was reported to the office of the District Attorney, the prosecutor told him "to take a vacation until this whole thing blows over."

All of the students who testified said they had witnessed the beating of Stewart, but they were unable to identify the police officer(s) responsible for the acts. A physician, Dr. Marie Crocetti, who lived in the non-student section of the dormitory, testified that she, too, had witnessed the beating.

A registered nurse from Bellevue Hospital testified that when Stewart was wheeled into the emergency room he had bruises all over his body and was not breathing. Lillian Conrad said she noticed numerous skin abrasions, discoloration on the wrist and neck, and blue splotches above his eyes. "I could tell he wasn't breathing because I couldn't feel any air," she maintained. "After he was turned over I could really see. There was no rise or fall in his chest, which indicates if someone is breathing or not." She continued, "I turned his head so he could get air, so he could possibly breathe, then started running with the stretcher to the resuscitation room." She then testified that attempts to revive and treat Stewart were delayed because he was handcuffed. Medical personnel at first tried to cut his clothing off but were hampered in this because police officers could not find the key for the handcuffs.

The physician who directed the emergency room team at Bellevue, Dr. David Pizutti, testified that when Stewart was wheeled into the emergency room he had no heartbeat, pulse, or blood pressure. A colleague, Dr. Duncan McBride, confirmed his testimony.

Chief Medical Examiner Dr. Elliot Gross' testimony was a textbook case study in perjury and corruption in high places. On the stand, he revealed that he had changed the autopsy report three times. In the first report, he had attributed Stewart's death to cardiac arrest; in the second report, he said it was caused by physical injury to the spinal cord. After he asked other pathologists, including Dr. Harry Zimmermann, to clarify the significance of the spinal injury, Gross revealed that he again revised his opinion of the cause of death.

When asked by the Assistant District Attorney in court, "Can you now formulate an opinion as to the cause of Michael Stewart's death, with a degree of medical certainty, based on the clinical records, the reports of the consultants and your own post-mortem examination?" Gross' answer was, "No, I cannot."

During his testimony, which lasted for two weeks, Gross gave a puzzling series of answers to questions. For example, on October 8, 1985, he testified that the injuries suffered by Stewart were not consistent with the actions of transit police officers as described in their testimony. He claimed that the injuries were consistent with the actions described by the many witnesses, who said they saw officers hit, kick, and put a choke-hold on Stewart. This time he said the injuries occurred as a result of "blunt-force trauma." The major injuries, he explained, represent "an application of force or of the deceased having struck an object." Again, he repeated that the injuries were consistent with the testimony of 23 witnesses who testified that they had observed transit police officers beating Stewart.

The next day Gross testified that a "combination of factors," including acute intoxication, effects of physical restraints and the infliction of "blunt force trauma," could have caused the death.

On October 15, Gross again said that Stewart's blood alcohol level could have contributed to his death. But a cardiologist from Harvard Medical School, Dr. Thomas Graboys, disputed the influence of alcohol in the death. He said Stewart had been beaten to death.

The Chief Medical Examiner of Massachusetts, Dr. Brian Blackbourne, testified on October 28 that choking caused Stewart's death. He said that his review of hospital records and the autopsy report indicated that Stewart died of asphyxia as a result of force applied to his neck.

By the end of the trial, Dr. Gross was the subject of at least
five investigations on city, state, and federal levels. Furthermore, he had been forced at least twice to take leaves of absence
from his duties, and the New York State Board of Professional
Medical Conduct had pronounced him incompetent. Finally,
he was removed from his position by the Mayor in October
1987.

Defense attorneys decided not to call witnesses; the
prosecution rested its case. There seemed little doubt that,
based on the evidence, the transit officers would be convicted.
Rarely had so many witnessed a beating and agreed to come
forward and testify. Nonetheless, it is especially difficult to
convict officers, particularly those responsible for murdering
Black people.

As one might expect, despite the evidence, the jury, which
did not include any Black people, acquitted all of the police
officers of all charges after deliberating for nearly seven days.
Thus ended the trial, which had lasted for five months. When
the verdict was handed down, a mass demonstration erupted
outside the court. Concerned citizens were outraged that the
jury had failed to convict the police officers in the face of all the
evidence presented.

AFTERMATH OF THE TRIAL

The verdict of the jury became part of the controversy
surrounding the death of Michael Stewart. Indeed, two of the
jurors, Peter Griffin and Richard Essex, wrote an article for the

New York Times that was published several weeks after the trial in a bizarre attempt to explain their vote. They explained away virtually all of the eyewitness accounts and the plethora of medical evidence, saying that the witnesses who saw the beating "did not describe it as sustained." They wrote that they understood Stewart's injuries upon arrival at Bellevue Hospital as "superficial cuts and bruises." The evidence, they maintained, "did not support the charge that Mr. Stewart was beaten or strangled." Their strange article appears to be part of what the Stewart family lawyer rightfully called a cover-up. Clearly, the two jurors were trying to justify their decisions in this controversial case. Their "explanation" only serves to reinforce the strong feelings shared by many in the Black community that police brutality is rampant and that white police officers will not be convicted of their crimes, whatever the evidence.

The U.S. Attorney in New York, Rudolph Guiliani, announced that he would investigate the death of Michael Stewart. However, in July 1986, federal prosecutors declared that there was insufficient evidence to warrant a federal grand jury investigation into the death of Michael Stewart. Guiliani maintained that there were "major inconsistencies" in the accounts of witnesses and that the medical evidence on the cause of death was inconclusive.

In January 1987, the Michael Stewart case took yet another turn. When the trial ended, the mayor, not considered to be a champion of the rights of Black people, said he felt that the "criminal courts have not done their job" and called for further investigation into the case. In this regard, he showed greater insight than the two jurors who explained away the brutality of the police officers. The Transit Authority then hired Harold Tyler Jr., a retired federal judge, as Special Counsel to conduct a renewed investigation and determine if departmental charges should be filed against the transit officers.

The report of the Special Counsel, issued one year after its inception, declared that the transit police officers involved were guilty of using excessive restraint and that John Kostick had lied when he testified that he saw Michael Stewart breathing while taking him to Bellevue Hospital. The report was especially critical of James Meehan, the transit authority chief, noting that, "By the early morning of September 15, it was obvious that a major and extraordinary tragedy had occurred," and that Meehan "did nothing to investigate the tragedy, or to see that anyone else did." Furthermore, the report stated that restraining Stewart "with his wrists bound to his ankles in a 'hog-tied' position, was unwarranted in the circumstances here, where there were at least 11 officers in the immediate vicinity available to assure that he did not injure a police officer, a civilian or himself." Finally, the report charged the arresting officer with "dereliction of duty" because he failed to monitor Stewart's condition as he was driven to the hospital.

However, the only recommendation made in the report was that disciplinary proceedings be initiated against John Kostick, the arresting officer, for giving false testimony. This is surprising because the report found that excessive force had been used in arresting Stewart.

Shortly after the Tyler report was issued, the chairman of the Metropolitan Transportation Authority appointed a three-member panel to consider what disciplinary steps, if any, should be taken, and what changes needed to be made in procedures for investigating such cases.

The panel issued its report in March 1987 and recommended that John Kostick face departmental perjury charges, but two of the three members concluded that "it would be fruitless" to recommend disciplinary proceedings against the other 10 officers because of contradictory testimony from witnesses. The panel agreed that "Mr. Stewart stopped breathing some time before his arrival at the hospital," although Kostick had testified that he saw him breathing while in the van. The one Black member of the panel, Laura Blackburne, recommended that all 11 officers be charged with using excessive force and making false oral reports.

The report of the three-member panel was sent to the board of the transit authority. The board decided that 10 of the transit officers should be charged with Michael Stewart's murder and that John Kostick should face perjury charges. The board voted 7 to 5 against charging the officers with the use of excessive force and 8 to 3 against charging them with official misconduct.

The transit authority then hired an outside law firm to prosecute the case against John Kostick in order to avoid the appearance of bias. The outside firm, Anderson, Russell, Kill and Olick, submitted its report in October 1987, in which it concluded that it "would be virtually impossible to prove" that Kostick had lied when he claimed he heard Michael Stewart breathing while being transported to Bellevue Hospital. According to its report, only one of seven medical experts consulted during the preparations for the case corroborated the finding that Stewart had stopped breathing approximately 15 minutes before his arrival at the hospital. The other doctors, according to the report, had concluded that "it was certainly medically possible that Stewart was breathing in the van, and that some of the doctors offered scenarios that would support Mr. Kostick's account." The board then voted 7 to 1 to withdraw the departmental charges. The one Black member of the Board, vice chairman Lawrence Bailey, voted against dropping the charge.

The Stewart family sued for $40 million, charging that Stewart's death resulted from the excessive use of force by the police. They also charged that city officials had engaged in a cover-up for the transit police.

Seven years after the death of Michael Stewart, his family won a settlement of $1.7 million in damages. The settlement between the Stewart family and 15 defendants, including the City of New York, the Metropolitan Transportation Authority, the 11 transit police officers, the former Chief Medical Examiner and the former transit police chief, was approved in Federal District Court in Manhattan on August 28, 1990.

When the settlement was announced, a lawyer for the union of transit police officers said, "There is no admission of wrong-doing by any transit officer in the suit." But in approving the settlement, Judge Miriam Cedarbaum stated that "agreed arrangements are often more just than judgements after trial."

There are some who would maintain that justice has been served in the Michael Stewart case, but the view still held among Blacks is that he was killed by the transit police officers. It is because of incidents like the Michael Stewart case that, in minority communities across the country, there remains the view that police misconduct against minorities is widespread and that any police officer who kills a Black person will be cleared of criminal charges. The case of Michael Stewart supports this contention.

7

ELEANOR BUMPERS: GRANDMOTHER

OVERVIEW

"The police are at war with our people. No White officer has ever been convicted for killing a Black person. [Judge Fred W.] Eggert's decision was consistent with history," concluded Attorney Colin Moore after attending the trial at which a white policeman, Stephen Sullivan, was acquitted in the shooting death of a 66-year-old, ailing Black grandmother, Eleanor Bumpers. Bumpers suffered from swollen feet, arthritis, high blood pressure and a cardiac condition. The murder occurred on October 29, 1984, when six police officers broke into Bumpers' New York City-owned apartment in the Bronx to evict her because she was four months late in paying the $96.85 monthly rent. When Eleanor Bumpers resisted, the police pumped two blasts from a 12-gauge shotgun into her body. Eleanor Bumpers died on the way to Lincoln Hospital in the Bronx.

Few violent crimes against Black people in New York City's history caused as much anger and apprehension in the Black community as the shooting death of Eleanor Bumpers. The non-jury trial took place in the midst of a rash of racist attacks on Black people by police and citizens alike.

There was the Howard Beach case, in which a mob of white youths drove a Black man to his death on a widely traveled highway and beat two others without provocation. New York City transit police had fatally beaten Michael Stewart, a 25-year-old Black artist, for writing graffiti on a subway wall. This incident brought about the resignation of the chief of the transit police, James Meehan. These are but two of the many cases that created consternation in the Black community. Given the hostile climate, it should not have been surprising to anyone that the frustration of New York's Black community would erupt into massive demonstrations when the verdict was announced on February 26, 1987. After the acquittal verdict, Officer Sullivan proclaimed, "I was very happy, very pleased. I had no doubt about it. Like I said before, I never felt that I was guilty. It was a job I had to do, and I don't think I'd change it at all."

Members of the Patrolmen's Benevolent Association (PBA) had been demonstrating their support for Sullivan since the indictment was announced by the Bronx District Attorney.

Thousands of white police officers marched in protest before the announcement. On the day of the verdict, the PBA (the police union) packed the courtroom with its members, denying seats to the many African Americans who had appeared at the courthouse. Outside, the police department stationed more than 200 officers in and around the courthouse and positioned two police helicopters on the roof. When the acquittal verdict was announced, hundreds of police officers cheered loudly and embraced each other. They held a victory celebration in the courthouse.

THE ACCOUNT

According to the police, at about 9:30am on October 29, 1984, a city marshall, accompanied by Housing Authority officers, went to Eleanor Bumpers' apartment to evict her for non payment of rent. She refused to let them in and made threats through the locked door. The city police were then notified, and five members of the Emergency Service Unit (who are specially trained to deal with emotionally disturbed people) responded. The number of people present to evict the aging grandmother stood at six.

The officers punched out the lock on the door and entered the apartment, carrying hard plastic shields designed to protect against blows and knife thrusts. They also carried a U-shaped "restraining" bar attached to a long handle that is used to pin a person. The officers were also equipped with chemical mace, but did not use it.

The police maintained that they tried to restrain Bumpers, and that Sullivan fired his shotgun when she lunged at one of the officers with a knife. In what some considered to be a shocking admission, when asked why Sullivan had not fired a warning shot, Deputy Police Chief John P. Lowe replied, "Our officers are not allowed to fire warning shots. They are trained to hit the target, not a leg or an arm, but the main part of the body."

The slain woman's daughter, Mary, questioned the police account of the murder. In an interview she said that her mother suffered from high blood pressure and arthritis. "And she had trouble moving quickly. Shotguns are for elephant hunting, not for an old woman who was terrified by people breaking into her apartment. They were there to kill her, not to subdue her." She explained that she and other relatives had advised her mother, who lived alone, not to allow strangers into the apartment. "We told her, 'Mom, don't open the door for nobody.' When they busted the door open, of course she got terrified and picked up a butcher knife. What would any old woman have done?"

The deputy police chief testified that Eleanor Bumpers was about to stab policeman John Elter when Sullivan fired his shotgun. He claimed that, upon looking through the hole the officers had punched in the top lock, they could see that she Bumpers had a knife in her hand. However, he contended, they did not use the chemical spray to subdue her because the building would have had to have been evacuated.

A neighbor of Eleanor Bumpers, Victor Garcia, said he looked through the peephole in his apartment door directly across the hall and saw the police enter Bumpers' apartment and shoot her. Contrary to the official account, he said he heard no warning from the police. Minutes after the shooting, he said he was in the hall, but the police did not question him. The only voice he heard was that of the victim, saying, ". . .Get out, get out, leave me alone."

The police initially reported that one shot had been fired on the day of the eviction attempt. But when the autopsy was performed on November 26, it showed that Eleanor Bumpers had been hit by two shotgun blasts. Nine pellets struck her in the chest, and one struck her on the hand. According to the autopsy report, she suffered "extensive destruction." Not surprisingly, when that information was released to the public, the police changed their story. They now maintained that the bullet that struck the hand that held the knife "had no effect on her charge," making a second shot necessary. Given the propensity of the police for perjury, what exactly happened that morning may never be known.

It is known, however, that the Chief Medical Examiner ordered the first autopsy reports altered to allow the possibility that Eleanor Bumpers had been struck by only one blast. Dr. Elliot Gross has been charged many times with altering autopsy reports to protect the police. His autopsy report in the Michael Stewart case (see Chapter 6) is legend.

Although the police maintained at first that only one shot had been fired, those at the scene claimed the officer fired two shots from the 12-gauge shotgun. In a report to the Mayor three weeks later, Police Commissioner Benjamin Ward explained the need for two shots by saying that the first had apparently missed. The second shot, he said, tore into Eleanor Bumpers' right hand and chest, killing her. But the Associate Medical Examiner who performed the autopsy, Dr. Jon S. Pearl, maintained that his report the day after the death had shown beyond doubt that both shots had hit the victim. Dr. Pearl later testified that Dr. Gross had called him at least three times with the same question: How many shots struck Eleanor Bumpers? "Every time I gave an absolutely clear answer that she was shot twice," he said.

In his report, Dr. Pearl listed the cause of death as "shotgun wounds (two) of chest, hand and lungs." He said it was his custom to always include the number of shots in parenthesis to avoid confusion. "Dr. Gross had never questioned it before," he said. This time, however, Dr. Gross instructed Dr. Pearl to change the finding to "shotgun wound to chest and lung, shotgun wound of hand" – without the number.

THE TRIAL

During the trial, Stephen Sullivan defended his decision to shoot Bumpers twice. Sullivan said of the first shotgun blast: "I thought I missed, because nothing changed. She still held the knife and was still flailing." He continued, "When I entered I observed Police Officer [George] Adams. She was slashing him. She had him down on one knee and was trying to get over the shield. She was right on top of him." He maintained that she next turned to Officer John Elter, who was trying to control her with the restraining bar. "She was slashing away. I feared for his life." He testified that after the first shotgun blast, he issued more warnings, but Bumpers did not desist, requiring him to fire again. Sullivan testified that after the second blast, she was "very surprised and stopped flailing." She then "took three or four steps to the left and went into the kitchen."

This testimony has been reproduced in some detail because some physicians and others have maintained that it was impossible for the events to have occurred as the police reported them, because the first blast would have knocked the knife from her hand, as it severed two of her fingers, making it unnecessary to fire a second blast. It would have been anatomically impossible for Eleanor Bumpers to have responded in the manner described by Sullivan.

Dr. Harold Osborn of Lincoln Hospital treated Eleanor Bumpers in the emergency room. Dr. Osborn maintained that "police officials continue to misrepresent the medical facts of the shooting." He wrote that the first of two shotgun blasts "tore off Mrs. Bumpers' right hand." Under questioning by Sullivan's attorney, Dr. Osborn acknowledged that only two fingers of Eleanor Bumpers' hand had been severed, but he insisted that two other fingers and part of the palm had been severely damaged as well. He described the hand as "a bloody stump." Waving a color photograph of Eleanor Bumpers' arm, Dr. Osborn said, "It has no anatomical integrity whatsoever." Finally, when asked by the prosecution whether it was possible for her to have attacked the officers after the first shot, he said, "It was anatomically impossible for this hand to hold this knife."

However, two doctors who never examined the victim maintained in court that it was possible for Eleanor Bumpers to continue to slash at police, even after the shotgun blast had torn away the part of her hand that held the knife. The two plastic surgeons, Jane A. Petro and William K. Boss, testified for Sullivan at his trial. According to Dr. Petro, "there was no apparent damage to the part of the hand that controls the power of grip," the small and ring fingers. Dr. Boss maintained that the fourth and fifth fingers of the victim's right hand appeared intact and that "she would have been physically able to hold a knife." Although both of these "expert" witnesses hold reputable positions in their fields, because they never saw the victim their testimony must be suspect. Furthermore, Drs. Boss and Petro were paid $750 each to testify for Sullivan. Paid witnesses have been known to say anything their benefactors tell them to say. In some circles, such "witnesses" are known as prostitutes.

Eleanor Bumpers' emotional problems were frequently reported during the trail, but members of her family denied these charges. Before the grand jury, a psychiatrist who had seen the victim prior to her death testified that Bumpers had been "psychotic" and "[did] not know reality from nonreality." At a news conference during which community leaders demanded an independent investigation into the death, a New York City Council member, Wendell Foster, alleged, "Every time a minority is killed in this city, the police say he was deranged or psychotic."

Although Police Commissioner Ward repeatedly maintained that departmental guidelines had been followed, on November 1, 1984, he ordered a major revision of the rules governing the disarming of emotionally disturbed people. The new procedure states that if an emotionally disturbed person poses no immediate threat, officers should take no action until a precinct commander or deputy captain is called to evaluate the situation and decide how the person should be restrained. Previously, a sergeant was in charge of such cases.

Eleanor Bumpers was buried on November 3, 1984. The funeral was attended by hundreds of people, including actors, clergy, community leaders, and family members. During his eulogy, Reverend Herbert Daughtry asked, "How long will the people paid to protect us continue to kill us?"

Even Police Commissioner Ward, the first Black person to hold that post, released a public statement. When asked how he would have restrained Eleanor Bumpers, he said, "Mrs. Bumpers and I have more in common than just being homo sapiens on the planet earth. We have some other things in common, including skin color, and probably some other type of heritage. For me to take that woman down with but one knife as opposed to taking seven steps back, I suspect I would have stepped outside the apartment and re-secured the door." But the Commissioner steadfastly maintained that Sullivan acted within police departmental guidelines.

In an editorial, the *New York Times* posed several questions: "Why couldn't six specially trained officers control an elderly, impaired woman? Did the kitchen knife she wielded give her that much of an advantage? Why didn't the commanding sergeant simply order a retreat as Police Commissioner Ward now suggests he would have done?"

Meanwhile, the Mayor of New York City, who did not attend the funeral but who attended all funerals for police officers killed on duty, paid an unexpected visit to Mary Bumpers on Thanksgiving Day. Officer Sullivan was transferred.

Because of the publicity surrounding the case, the U. S. Attorney in New York, Rudolph Guiliani, announced that the Federal Bureau of Investigation had commenced a civil rights investigation into the fatal shooting of Eleanor Bumpers. He maintained that the investigation was a routine one.

The Patrolmen's Benevolent Association commenced an advertising campaign on December 12, 1984, to counteract what it maintained was unfair criticism in the shooting death of Eleanor Bumpers. A spokesman for the 18,000-member group said the union would spend about $30,000 in a two-week period for advertisements on radio stations and in two mass-circulation newspapers. (Black members denounced this expenditure of union funds, to no avail.) In its commercials the union asserted: "This 300-pound woman suddenly charged one of the officers with a 12-inch butcher knife, striking the shield with so much force that it bent the tip of the steel blade. It was as she was striking again that the shots were fired. It happened so quickly they had no chance to subdue her – no chance." This commercial appeared while the grand jury was investigating the case, which caused some to question the motives of the PBA. In response to this advertisement, the *New York Times* editorialized that "the officers are determined to blame the dead victim."

On January 31, 1985, Stephen Sullivan was indicted for manslaughter by a grand jury. He pleaded not guilty and was released without bail. According to Bronx District Attorney Mario Merola, a person is guilty of manslaughter if he "recklessly causes the death of another person." Morola claimed that the key evidence in favor of the indictment was that Sullivan shot twice. The president of the PBA protested the indictment with the following statement: "[Sullivan] is being made a scapegoat for the failure to deal with a tragedy of this magnitude." Police Commissioner Ward ordered Sullivan suspended without pay. When she learned that the indictment charged Sullivan with manslaughter rather than murder, Bumpers' daughter remarked, "My mother is gone forever and they're talking about 15 years [for Sullivan]."

Police Commissioner Ward repeated his charge that Sullivan had acted within departmental guidelines. To this, the District Attorney remarked, "Hitler's people also followed guidelines. You can't just follow orders blindly and escape your individual responsibility."

In response to the indictment, thousands of police officers demonstrated to show support for Sullivan. All of the 250 officers in the Emergency Service Unit demanded transfers in protest. The demonstrating police officers were especially angry with the District Attorney. During the demonstration they shouted, "Merola must go." At about the same time, the Mayor raised questions about the indictment and declared publicly that he disagreed with the grand jury. On February 10, 1985, it was announced that Sullivan would ask for a bench trial.

On April 12, 1985, a state judge, Acting Justice Vincent Vitale of the State Supreme Court, dismissed the manslaughter charge against Sullivan, citing insufficient evidence. The judge claimed Sullivan's actions were in accord with police policy. Police Commissioner Ward announced that he agreed with the dismissal of the indictment.

The dismissal of the indictment against Sullivan was affirmed by the Appellate Division of the State Supreme Court on April 1, 1986. When the decision was handed down, the District Attorney announced that the case would be appealed to the State's highest court, the New York Court of Appeals.

Later that year, on November 25, the Court of Appeals reinstated the manslaughter charge against Sullivan. In its decision, the Court cited conflicting testimony about the number of seconds between the two shotgun blasts fired by the officer, the second of which killed Eleanor Bumpers.

The 6-1 ruling reversed the two lower court decisions that had vacated the second-degree manslaughter indictment pronounced by the Bronx grand jury in January 1985. As a result, Sullivan was required to stand trial on the manslaughter charge. In the lone dissent, Chief Justice Sol Wachtler rejected the manslaughter charge as too lenient; rather, he said, the evidence warranted either of the more serious charges of second-degree murder or first-degree manslaughter.

In its majority opinion, the Court of Appeals stated that, "The question to be resolved in this case involves the defendant's second shot, which led to Mrs. Bumpers' death." Sullivan, the opinion read, testified before a grand jury "that the first shot did not seem to deter Mrs. Bumpers and that she continued to approach the downed officer with her knife. Thus, he testified, a second later, he fired the second shot. While the testimony of most observers corroborated this account, one witness estimated that the second shot was fired as many as five seconds later." The opinion also pointed to the medical testimony that the first shot had blown off the thumb and index fingers of the hand in which Eleanor Bumpers was holding the knife, rendering her incapable of harming the downed officer. The court ruled that there was sufficient evidence to warrant a trial on the second-degree manslaughter charge.

In his dissent, Judge Wachtler declared that the grand jury should have charged Sullivan with "a reckless shooting," stating that an indictment based on an "intentional shooting" would have been warranted. The evidence presented to the grand jury "would have supported an indictment for murder or manslaughter based on an intentional shooting." He concluded, "In my view, the indictment charging the defendant with a reckless shooting is a compromise with no support in evidence."

According to the District Attorney, the issue was "whether the police officer used reasonable force or whether he used excessive force." He continued, "Obviously, one shot would have been justified. But if that shot took off part of her hand, and rendered her defenseless, whether there was any need for a second shot, which killed her, that's the whole issue of whether you have reasonable force or excessive force."

In an editorial, the *New York Times* welcomed the Court of Appeals decision to reinstate the manslaughter charge against Sullivan. "Controversy centered on whether the second, probably fatal, shot to Mrs. Bumpers' chest was necessary. Yet it has never been resolved, because two lower courts ruled that the evidence was legally insufficient to support the indictment. Now the state's highest court rightfully reverses that judgement, focusing on the second shot." The editorial continued, "How much discipline can reasonably be expected from a police officer in such a situation? That important question has remained unanswered, and the impression lingers that fear of a police revolt caused the lower courts to duck the issue . . . As the Court of Appeals has now recognized, this is precisely the kind of question that can best be answered by a jury, not the politics of policy-community relations."

Amid massive protests from the police, the Sullivan trial commenced on January 12, 1987, in a courtroom filled with angry Black citizens. As had been suspected, the trial went before Judge Fred W. Eggert with no jury. As the defense lawyer, Bruce Smithy, began his opening statement, a chorus of voices erupted from the Black spectators. They shouted "liar" and "cover-up," and the boos were so loud that the defense lawyer was forced to halt his presentation. Later, while a witness was being questioned, five men walked to the front of the courtroom and unfurled a white sheet with a picture of Eleanor Bumpers on it. The spectators cheered as the men were escorted from the courtroom.

The defense attorney asserted that the family of the deceased shared responsibility for her death. "If members of the deceased's family had complied with their family obligations," the death might have been averted, he said to a chorus of jeers from the spectators who perceived this remark as blaming the victim.

In his opening statement, prosecuting attorney Lawrence Lebowitz asserted that the first shot tore away most of Eleanor Bumpers' right hand and that she was no longer a threat to the officers.

Herman Ruiz, a city social worker, was the first witness to be called to the stand. Ruiz testified that, from the vestibule outside Bumpers' apartment, he saw police break into the apartment. He said he heard a commotion like a "struggle or a fight," and one of the police officers was saying, "Make it drop. Take it off of her." He said he then heard a shot, followed by another, one or two seconds later.

The police officer whom Sullivan said he sought to protect, John Elter, testified that he did not see whether Bumpers was still holding the knife after the first shot. Elter estimated that the time lapse between the two shotgun blasts was "almost a second or a second." Before entering the apartment he said the police, looking through a hole in the door, saw the elderly woman holding a knife. They repeatedly asked her to drop it, he testified. As police entered the apartment, Elter said he "placed the [restraining] bar in her mid-section and she started slashing at me." He testified that she continued to make stabbing motions before the second shot was fired.

During the trial, crucial testimony came from Dr. Osborn, the emergency room physician who treated Eleanor Bumpers immediately after the shooting. He maintained that after the first shot, the right hand was a "bloody stump" that had "no anatomical integrity whatsoever." Drs. Boss and Petro, the two paid "expert" witnesses, testified, without having examined the body, that Eleanor Bumpers could have continued to slash at police officers even after the first shotgun blast had torn away part of her hand.

The presentation of testimony at the trial lasted for six weeks. During the summations, the defense attorney accused the daughter of Eleanor Bumpers of lying during her testimony. The spectators in the courtroom shouted, "Convict Stephen Sullivan!" "Sullivan murderer!" and "Sullivan guilty!" The demonstrators, members of the Eleanor Bumpers Justice Committee, refused to quiet down or leave, forcing the judge to recess the trial. During the demonstration, Reverend Herbert Daughtry read a list of names of Blacks and Hispanics who had been killed by police. After 25 minutes, the demonstration subsided. When the prosecutor presented his closing argument, he dismissed the argument of family indifference, ineptitude by the medical team, and bureaucratic muddling by city agencies. In response to the defense argument that Sullivan was doing what he had been trained to do, the prosecution described him as a "robot." "He would have fired again, until he got the result he was programmed to expect." Responding to the defense argument that the Emergency Service Unit of which Sullivan was a member was an elite unit with great responsibility, prosecutor Lebowitz said, "Doing it 100 times right doesn't make-up for one time wrong. And you have to stand and face the music when you do it wrong."

As promised, Judge Eggert reconvened the trial on February 26 to announce his verdict. As is typical in such cases (a white policeman killing a Black citizen), few people were surprised when Stephen Sullivan was cleared of all charges in connection with the death of Eleanor Bumpers. According to the judge, the prosecution had failed to prove "beyond a reasonable doubt" that Sullivan's second shot was "legally unjustifiable" and that his actions had been "a gross deviation from the standard of conduct a reasonable police officer would be expected to follow." He thus found Sullivan not guilty of second-degree manslaughter and of criminally negligent homicide, a lesser charge. As the judge began reading his verdict, a spectator from the Eleanor Bumpers Justice Committee demanded either that more people from the community be allowed in the courtroom or that the proceedings be moved to a larger room. He was dragged from the courtroom by six officers.

THE AFTERMATH

In the halls of the building and outside, hundreds of protesters, fearing that Sullivan would be acquitted, demonstrated angrily. In an editorial following the verdict, the *New York Times*, while agreeing with Judge Eggert, raised some humanitarian questions: "Why did they [the police] carry a shotgun to enforce a civil eviction order? And when Mrs. Bumpers threatened them, why didn't they simply retreat and wait for her to leave or agree to talk with her?"

Reverend Daughtry summed up the feelings of most people in the Black community when he said, "This is the same thing that happened with Michael Stewart, Randolph Evans and other victims of police murder. We must go back and organize; everyone should join an organization and keep fighting for political and economic power and justice."

Attorney William Kunstler believed that the case had not been properly presented by the Bronx District Attorney and that he had, "in effect, throw[n] the case." He criticized the District Attorney for assigning the trial to an inexperienced assistant and failing to adequately prepare and interview witnesses for cross-examination. He also criticized the judge for his conservative and pro-police leanings. As Kunstler declared, "In short, it was obvious to me, as well as to many observers, that the system was looking for anything but a conviction in this case. If nothing else, the inevitable outcome demonstrates the wisdom of Attorneys Alton Maddox and C. Vernon Mason in insisting on the appointment of a special prosecutor before permitting their clients in the Howard Beach case to cooperate with the Queens County District Attorney."

8

BERNHARD GOETZ: SUBWAY VIGILANTE

OVERVIEW

When Bernhard Goetz shot four Black teenagers on a Manhattan subway train on December 22, 1984, claiming that he thought they were going to rob him, he became an international celebrity. When the New York Police Department set up a hotline for information on the shooting, hundreds of callers praised Goetz, many offered to pay for his defense if he was arrested, some expressed disappointment that the teenagers were not killed, and others suggested that he should run for mayor.

This shooting took place in a climate of hostility against Black people: a transit worker had been murdered by a racist mob in Brooklyn; a young artist and model had been murdered by a mob of New York City transit authority police officers; and

155

a policeman had just murdered, without reason, a 66-year-old grandmother.

Furthermore, the Reagan administration had led the fight to roll back the small gains that Black people had made during the so-called Great Society period and the time of affirmative action. Greed, meanness, and self-interest were being celebrated in the United States as never before in modern times. Right-wing conservatives were enjoying widespread support throughout the country, in and out of government, and their public policy positions were being adopted and enacted into law. In other words, there were many indicators of widespread discontent with the aspirations of Black people that contributed to the nationwide climate of hostility. As has been contended, ordinary citizens were taking their cues from officials in the Reagan Administration. The mainstream support that this subway vigilante received from citizens was indicative of the country's dangerous conservative mood — a mood that had found a champion in Ronald Reagan.

THE ACCOUNT

According to the transit authority police report, the following events occurred during the early afternoon of December 22, 1984. At about 1:45pm, a middle-aged white man with a silver-colored pistol entered a subway car rolling through lower Manhattan and shot four young men he had apparently singled out from among the other passengers. "As the victims collapsed, all bleeding profusely from wounds of the upper body, a dozen other passengers, screaming and sobbing, fell on the floor or headed into the next car," reported the *New York Times*. "Then, in a bizarre twist to what transit authorities called one of the worst crimes of the year in the subways, the gunman discussed the shootings briefly with a conductor [on the train] according to investigators, one of whom described the colloquy: 'Are you a cop?' the conductor was said to have asked as he approached the man, who had shoved the gun into his waist band and was bending over and saying something to a victim." "No," the gunman replied. "They tried to rip me off."

Throughout, the gunman was described as "calm, cool and collected." He noticed two trembling women lying on the floor and, along with the conductor, helped them up. As the women fled to the next car, the conductor turned to the gunman and said, "Give me the gun," but the gunman turned without responding and stepped through the door at the end of the car. The conductor tried to grab him, but he leaped to the tracks and disappeared into the dark tunnel.

According to transit authority police officer John Kelly, "He picked out these four guys and shot every one of them. He knew what he was doing. He was not shooting indiscriminately. He was either harassed or robbed by these guys earlier on the train."

The wounded teenagers, who were all friends from the Bronx, were interviewed later the same day at Bellevue and St. Vincent's Hospitals. They denied either harassing or robbing the man who shot them. Three of the four had prior arrest records, and three of them were carrying long screwdrivers in their jackets.

At Bellevue Hospital, two of the victims – Barry Allen, 18, and James Ranseur, 18 – were listed in serious condition. At St. Vincent's Hospital, Darrell Cabey, 19, was in critical condition. A bullet had passed through his spinal cord and left lung. Troy Cantry, 19, was in serious condition, with a wound in the left side of the chest above the heart.

When the gunman entered the subway car, the four teenagers were seated near the rear – three on one side and one on the other. There were at least a dozen other people in the car, including an off-duty transit authority porter. One of the teenagers approached the gunman, asked for the time or a match, a cigarette, and then $5. The gunman then said, "Yes, I have five dollars for each of you." He then stood up and started shooting.

As he admitted later, the gunman leaned over one slumped youth and said, "You seem to be doing all right. Here's another." He then fired another shot at the youth, which left him crippled for life.

The transit authority employee who witnessed the episode, Victor Flores, said later, "The kids were frightened, backing off, trying to get away. There was no reason to shoot them. They fell, one after the other. Bang! Bang! Bang!"

When the subway train came to a stop before reaching the Chambers Street station, Goetz left and ran along the dark tunnel until he reached the subway station. He then exited, returned to his home, changed clothes, packed a bag, rented an automobile, and drove to Bennington, Vermont. While there, he telephoned a neighbor, Myra Friedman, and told her the story of what happened on the subway. He later moved to New Hampshire.

An anonymous caller telephoned the New York City police after a composite drawing had been circulated. The caller said that the drawing fit the description of Bernhard Goetz and warned that he was armed and dangerous.

On December 31, 1984, Goetz surrendered to police in Concord, New Hampshire. On January 1, 1985, he was charged as a fugitive and taken to the county jail in Boscanen, New Hampshire, where he was held in lieu of $500,000 bail. The fugitive charge stemmed from the possibility of his being indicted for attempted murder. Shortly after being jailed, Goetz told a judge in Concord, New Hampshire, that he would volun-tarily return to New York City to face attempted murder charges.

Goetz was returned by detectives to New York City where he was held on $50,000 cash bail and placed in protective custody at Rikers Island jail. There were several offers to post bail from his family, friends, and strangers; but he rejected them saying that he wanted to raise his own bail. A legal defense fund was established by the Guardian Angels (a vigilante group) whose members collected money in the subway.

In New York, Goetz was arraigned on charges of illegal possession of a gun and attempted murder. When these charges were presented to a grand jury on January 25 by District Attorney Robert Morgenthau, the jurors decided that he had been justified in the use of force and declined to indict him on any charges but illegal weapons possession. This decision was received with apprehension in some quarters, for it was felt that the District Attorney had not pursued the case with the vigor it demanded.

Although he had been known as shy, Goetz appeared to revel in his notoriety. He publicly called for other civilians to arm themselves, and whenever a police officer or a cab driver was killed, he dutifully appeared at the funerals as an act of solidarity. He granted interviews almost daily. Soon, news of his videotaped interview in New Hampshire, in which he described himself as a monster, was leaked. Public opinion was gradually turning against him; people began to question his behavior during and after the subway incident.

Bowing to public opinion, the District Attorney, who was up for re-election later in the year, announced that because new evidence had surfaced, a second grand jury would be convened. The second grand jury convened, and after eight days of deliberations, Goetz was indicted on charges of attempted murder and assault.

In the meantime, the Goetz case continued to be debated both nationally and internationally. The primary issues in the case appeared to be: When is the use of self-defense appropriate? Through whose eyes must that determination be made? Blacks wanted to know if the attack was racially motivated. Would Goetz have shot four white teenagers in comparable circumstances? Corollary questions were, What lesson did the shooting of four teenagers convey to the public in general? Was the public adulation of Goetz an indication of the increased racism permeating the United States as part of Ronald Reagan's backlash?

The debate continued to rage, and one year later, in January 1986, a State Supreme Court Justice, Stephen Crane, dismissed charges of attempted murder and assault against Bernhard Goetz. He cited prejudicial error by a prosecutor who had instructed the second grand jury as well as the strong possibility that two of the victims may have perjured themselves. The latter charge by the justice stemmed from public statements allegedly made by the two victims, one to a newspaper reporter and another to a police officer, in which they were said to have admitted that they had planned to rob Goetz. In what must be called a shocking abuse of judicial responsibility, the judge based this ruling on newspaper accounts. This controversial ruling led to charges of racism on the part of the judge. The judge did, however, permit charges of weapons possession and reckless endangerment to stand. Furthermore, he determined that the case could be presented to another grand jury.

Several days after Justice Crane's ruling, the District Attorney announced that he would appeal the case to the Appellate Division of the State Supreme Court because he believed the decision's "interpretation of the law [was] wrong and the dismissal [was] erroneous" and that the facts in the case should be litigated by a jury. On the question of self-defense, the District Attorney argued that justification would be made by standards of a reasonable person in the situation rather than by Goetz's subjective state of mind. The judge, who had dropped the major charges in the case, had argued that Goetz's own assessment of the situation should be the controlling factor.

. . .

When Goetz surrendered to the police in Concord, New Hampshire, police officers read to him the Miranda warning, explaining that he did not have to talk to police if he did not want to. However, Goetz claimed that he wanted to. During the next four hours, two of which were videotaped, Goetz recounted the circumstances in the shooting. His interview, striking for its bizarre and contradictory statements, shed some light on his troubled personality.

When asked whether the four people he shot were on the train when he entered, he said, "Oh, sure." He was then asked whether they were Black or white. "Well, they were four Black, four young Black men." "What did they say to you?" he was asked. "You see what they said wasn't even so much as important as the look, the look, you see the body language, you have to, you know, it's, uh, you know, that's what I call it, the body language." Finally, he said that one of them said, "Give me five dollars."

Later, he said that their look was menacing. "I looked, you see I looked at his face, and you know, his eyes were shiny. You know, he, he, he was, if you can believe that, his eyes were shiny, he was enjoying himself. You see, and then he had a big smile on his face . . . and at that point, you're in a bad situation, O.K.? . . . You know, it's kind of like a cat plays with a mouse before, you know, it's horrible, but, uh." Later, he continued, "It's the confrontation, that was the threat right there. It was seeing his smile and his eyes lit up and the presence of the four and I knew, I know my situation, I knew my situation."

Goetz was then asked what his intention was. "My intention was to do anything I could do to hurt them. My intention, you know, I know it sounds horrible, but my intention was to murder them, to hurt them, to make them suffer as much as possible."

Goetz was asked how he obtained the handgun. "I did purchase it legally in Florida. And look, I know I've broken many laws and rules, but I just want to tell you something. In New York, I feel, and a lot of people feel, you have to have a gun, but they don't let you, to them it is a big crime, they have you, also they have you trapped, you can't, you're in a situation where you must carry a gun."

Goetz went on to explain that after having been mugged earlier, he decided to carry a gun. "It [the mugging] taught me that, the city doesn't care what happens to you. You see, you don't know what it's like to be a victim inside. I, I, I want to explain something. It's taught me a lot of things, it taught me, the worst part of being attacked, really the worst part, is that you don't know, from moment, to moment, you don't know, you do not know what is going to happen the next moment, and you know anything can happen, and I mean anything, O.K.?"

When asked if he was afraid during the incident, Goetz said that he was not afraid of dying. "What I'm afraid of is being maimed and of, of these things happening slowly and not knowing what's going to happen from moment to moment. The fear, in this case, the fear is a funny thing, you see, this is really combat. That's what it is, it's the only word to describe it."

He then explained the order in which he shot the four teenagers, saying, ". . . they can accuse me, maybe what I did was irresponsible, too, but they can accuse me of being the, the, the coldest murderer they want, that's O.K., but at least I wasn't careless like some of the people in New York are now. There, there, there are people who are firing guns and they must not be thinking about what they're doing. It's crazy, I at least thought before. . . ."

He was then asked where he shot the first person, that is, to which part of the body he had fired. "The center of the body is the important thing. . . ." That is what he aimed for. He had aimed for the same spot with the second and third persons. He then asked the interviewing officer, "Does that sound horrible? O.K., O.K., it is, it's disgusting."

"What type of bullets were you using?" asked the officer. "O.K., O.K., let me explain. Two different types of rounds. What you have to do, and I know this is gonna sound so criminal, you need the maximum stopping power, and you use something that is highly illegal." Goetz then admitted that he had used non-ricocheting hollow ("dum-dum") bullets.

When asked again the order in which he shot the teenagers, he gave this lengthy answer. "What I did, and I know people are gonna say this is the most horrible thing, and I admit, for those guys, all this time I wanted to do the worst possible thing a human being could do. That you, that I, that I was capable of doing. I went back to the other, I spun and went back to the other two ... The guy who was standing up, or something like that, he was then sitting down. I wasn't sure if I had shot him before, because he just seemed O.K. Now I said I know this sounds, this is gonna sound vicious, and it is, I mean, how else can you describe it? I said, 'you seem to be all right, here's another.' Now, you see what happens is, I was gonna shoot him anyway, I'm sure, I had made up, I mean, in my mind that, I was gonna pull the trigger anyway, but he jerked his right arm and on reflex he was shot instantly."

Who is Bernhard Goetz? He was born in Queens, New York, on November 7, 1947, the youngest of four children — two boys and two girls. His father immigrated from Osnabruck, Germany, to the United States in 1928. Goetz's mother was Jewish, his father Lutheran.

Goetz's father worked for a bookbinding company in Queens, and after a few years, he owned the company. He moved the business and the family to predominantly German Rhinebeck, New York. There, he also ran a 300-acre dairy farm. While not rich, the Goetz family was prosperous.

The children attended local schools in Rhinebeck where young Bernhard was said to have been more interested in science than in sports. Those who knew him said that he was an obedient child and rarely caused problems at school or at home. The father was a strong disciplinarian, and the children communicated with him in writing, often apologizing for behavior he considered improper. In their letters, they always addressed him by title. Bernhard Goetz was close to his parents.

In 1960, after living in Rhinebeck for 11 years, the father was indicted on 18 counts of molesting two 15-year-old boys. A jury found him guilty of eight counts, and three years later, the Court of Appeals ordered a new trial. Rather than endure another trial, the father pleaded guilty to a reduced charge of disorderly conduct. But by then, life in Rhinebeck had become quite difficult for the children, especially young Bernhard and his sister, Bernice. Family elders attempted to cushion them from the scandal by sending them to the Institute auf 'dem Rosenberg in St. Gallen, Switzerland, where the younger Goetz spent his high school years. This was during the early 1960s, and school tuition was $12,000 yearly.

The family moved to Orlando, Florida, in 1963. There, the father developed a tract of 1,100 homes known as Park Manor. This business venture netted several million dollars; the homes sold for $75,000 to $90,000 each.

Upon graduation from high school, Bernard Goetz moved to Orlando in 1964. In 1965, Goetz enrolled at New York University where he majored in nuclear engineering; he graduated in 1970 with a bachelor's degree. Upon graduation, he returned to Orlando where he worked for the development company his father founded. Goetz's mother died in 1977. His father, who spent much of his fortune fighting an unknown illness, died in 1984 at the age of 78. The estate was divided among the four siblings.

Goetz did not want to be drafted into the Army during the height of the Vietnam War, so he successfully feigned mental illness and sought psychiatric help. In 1979, he entered into a brief and unhappy marriage. After the divorce, Goetz moved back to New York City, rented an apartment on the fringe of Greenwich Village and started his own business. He specialized in calibrating electronic equipment to manufacturing standards. This business was operated out of his one-bedroom apartment.

Neighbors in his building reported that Goetz began a crusade to clean up the neighborhood, a shabby commercial district consisting of discount clothing, furniture, and appliance stores. They said he led the movement to keep Blacks and Hispanics out of his building, frequently referring to them as "niggers" and "spics."

Approximately three years before the subway shootings in January 1981, Goetz had been mugged by three youths at a subway station. He suffered a torn cartilage in his knee as a result of having been pushed into a plate-glass window. His most bitter memory of the mugging was that he spent six hours in the police station while the suspect was released in three hours.

As a result of the incident, and because he often carried large sums of money to bid at auctions, Goetz applied for a pistol permit, but his application was rejected on grounds of insufficient need. He was angered by this rejection, and on a subsequent visit to his family in Orlando, he purchased a .38-caliber revolver.

Unlike the vigilante gunman, the young victims of Goetz's shooting spree were products of America's urban Black slum communities, having grown up on the city's rough streets where they were hardly considered human beings. Indeed, Mayor Koch regularly referred to such youngsters, who have been discarded by society, as "animals." Goetz's defense attorney, Barry Slotnick, repeatedly referred to the victims as "savages" and "vicious predators." However, the four young men are not atypical of Black and other minority youths found in urban areas throughout the United States. Certainly, they are considerably more numerous than either Black male high school or college graduates.

Although the four had criminal records at the time of the shooting, and indeed they were facing criminal charges when the shootings occurred, these young men were victims. Given their police records, it is understandable that the defense lawyers would attempt to put *them* on trial. But the four did not commit or attempt to commit crimes at the time in question.

THE TRIAL

The Goetz trial was delayed because Barry Slotnick, Goetz's chief defense attorney who had amassed a fortune defending gangsters and white-collar criminals, was busy defending the reputed mobster John Carneglia, a co-defendant of alleged crime boss John Gotti. Slotnick is one of a battery of New York lawyers known for their defense of organized crime figures and racist whites who attack Blacks. These right-wing lawyers appear to be comfortable in both situations. They invariably attempt to blame Black victims for acts by white criminals and appear to delight in portraying Blacks as less than human. It is not simply a defense strategy, as some apologists maintain. Rather, it is the product of right-wing ideology, a manifestation of the Reagan backlash.

Slotnick is a proponent of the right to bear arms, as he discussed in an address before a New York State affiliate of the National Rifle Association. Unable to defend themselves, he maintained that residents are under "house arrest." Expressing sympathy for ordinary citizens, he said, "I can afford two people walking behind me, with bazookas, but what about the people who can't afford that kind of protection?" He maintained that he was protected from some of the hazards of contemporary life because he had "a suburban home, a car and driver, a big dog, a burglar alarm and other forms of security."

The trial of the subway vigilante commenced on April 27, 1987, more than two years after the shooting, with the chief defense attorney telling the jury that he intended to prosecute the four youths on charges that they intended to rob his client. After the opening statements and other court preliminaries, the prosecution played for the jury the videotaped account of the shooting by Goetz.

Defense attorneys insisted that Goetz was being robbed at the time he shot the four teenagers. Their defense was based, in part, on self-defense, that is, Goetz was justified in the shooting because he *thought* the victims were about to rob him. The prosecution maintained, however, that "reasonableness" goes beyond the victim's state of mind and that the self-defense justification must be an objective one. Was Goetz's conduct that of a reasonable person in that particular situation? That was the issue. As the District Attorney said when he appealed the ruling by the judge that dismissed charges of attempted murder and assault, "A subjective standard [of self-defense] justifies any use of deadly physical force even under circumstances which almost anyone in the community would think inappropriate. We do not believe the code of the Old West is appropriate in New York City in 1986." He continued, "The subjective standard could function to excuse a hot-tempered individual who rashly uses deadly force, so long as there is some reason for his action. Indeed, the publicity generated by this case alone would provide any subway rider with a 'reason' – and a license – to shoot when approached and panhandled by more than one Black youth."

While Goetz's attorneys announced that they would be "prosecuting" the four shooting victims on robbery charges in the course of defending the vigilante, the prosecutor in the case, Gregory Waples, countered that the defendant was "an emotional powder keg one spark away from a violent explosion." He charged that Goetz had shot the four young men out of a "twisted, self-righteous sense of right and wrong" and because "they were the type of people he hated with an all-consuming passion." The shooting was, he maintained, a "cold-blooded execution or attempted execution."

One of the first persons to testify at the trial was the paramedic who claimed to have heard one of the victims say that the four had been "hassling" Goetz for money. The paramedic, John Filangeri, testified that while taking Darrell Cabey from the scene of the shooting to the hospital, he asked the victim what had happened in the subway car. "These guys and I were hassling this guy for some money. He threatened us, then shot us." Although the paramedic testified that Cabey was apparently lucid when he made the statement, the victim was brain damaged and paralyzed from the waist down as result of the shooting. The testimony of this witness, which was not heard by the jury, indicates the extent to which public opinion in this case was supportive of the shooting.

Three of the people who were in the subway car with Goetz and his four victims at the time of the shooting testified for the prosecution. None of the three had seen the four youths surround Goetz as he had maintained. They testified, however, that they had been frightened even before the shooting. To be frightened in the New York subway is not uncommon, and the presence of four Black youth compounds the apprehension that some passengers feel.

Of the four persons shot, two were granted immunity from prosecution for their testimony, one invoked the Fifth

Amendment and refused to testify, and the fourth was hospital-ized because of brain damage and paralysis. Troy Cantry, who had asked Goetz for $5 on the subway train, testified that he had simply asked Goetz, "Mister, can I have $5?" The defense had attempted to prove that a demand – not a request – had been made.

James Ramseur, who had also been granted immunity from prosecution, refused to testify when first summoned. He refused to place his hand on the Bible for the witness' oath, and he refused to be sworn in. He simply said, "I refuse to take the stand." When the judge again ordered him to take the oath, he said, "I refuse." The judge then cited him for contempt. His attorney, Ronald Klingerman, said Ramseur had indicated that he might not testify but had apparently made up his mind at the last minute.

Two weeks later, Ramseur agreed to testify after the judge informed him that his cooperation would clear him of the previous contempt charge. However, Ramseur became angry with Slotnick's interrogation and finally refused to respond to further questions. The judge again cited him for contempt. When he did answer questions, he demonstrated his contempt for Slotnick. For example, when asked about his activities in the days before the subway shooting, Ramseur replied, "It's none of your business." He continued, "He's twisting things around and I don't like it." He later said to the judge, "The decision is made already. Take me out of here."

In another exchange, Slotnick asked Ramseur, "When was the last time you committed a crime?" Ramseur answered,

"When was the last time you got a drug dealer off?" "Mr. Ramseur, have we ever met?" Slotnick asked. "No, but I've heard about you," the witness responded. "I hope it was nothing unpleasant," Slotnick said. "It was unpleasant. I know about you, baby," Ramseur retorted.

The final youth to be called, Barry Allen, had not received immunity from prosecution. Rather than answer questions, Allen asserted his Fifth Amendment right against self-incrimination. Whenever a question was posed to him, he simply read from a prepared statement and refused to answer.

When Goetz's lawyers presented their defense of the vigilante, they were challenged with the videotape of Goetz's own admission that he was "a cold-blooded murderer," as well as an eyewitness' testimony that Goetz had deliberately taken aim and shot a helpless young man who was seated in the subway car. After his videotaped confession, Goetz had become angry each time he was asked a question by Assistant District Attorney Susan Braver. He squirmed, shouted, became vulgar, and finally yelled that he could not tolerate "Manhattan accents." This incident caused many people to question his sanity and the notion that his behavior had been "reasonable" under the circumstances.

The prosecutor had already described him as an "emotionally troubled" individual, one who had attempted a "cold-blooded execution" out of a "twisted, self-righteous sense of right and wrong." Goetz had admitted that he "snapped" when he saw the eyes of the youth who had asked him for $5.

173

The defense attorneys urged the jury to "forget the evidence" because the four people who had been shot all had criminal records. The jury should focus on their past behavior, the lawyers maintained. During his final appeal, Slotnick urged the jury not to believe the words of his own client. He said that Goetz's taped account was a "fantasy" and that his client was traumatized at the time. He maintained that the incident could not have happened the way Goetz himself had described it.

Slotnick presented a large blown-up poster of the four victims and declared, "It's these four who have distorted and destroyed [Goetz's] life. I ask you to put an end to that suffering." He maintained that one of the victims, Darrell Cabey, whose spine had been severed by the last bullet and who is permanently paralyzed and brain damaged, could not have been shot the way Goetz had described it on the videotape.

In his summation, prosecutor Gregory Waples urged the jurors to discard any sympathy they might have for Goetz and to submit the trial's evidence "to the acid test of logic." He told them to decide the case with their heads, not their hearts. The jurors were also asked to discard any antipathy they might have felt for the four youths shot in the case. Waples called Goetz "a very disturbed human being. He's the perfect example of the person who should not be carrying a gun in New York City." He reminded them of Goetz's calculated statement to Darrell Cabey as he lay injured, "You look all right, here's another." Then Waples said, "No matter how much you may sympathize with the defendant, you cannot wink at this 'you look all right; here's another' fifth shot. Darrell Cabey cries out for justice."

174

BERNHARD GOETZ: SUBWAY VIGILANTE

The jury, consisting of 2 Blacks and 10 whites, received the case on June 12, 1987. It had taken two-and-a-half years for the case to come to trial, and the trial lasted seven weeks. Judge Stephen Crane had told the jurors that to acquit Goetz, they had to be convinced on several levels that the force he used was neither excessive nor irrational.

On June 16, the jury announced that they found Goetz not guilty of attempted murder, assault, reckless endangerment, and the more serious gun possession charges. Altogether, there had been 13 charges against Goetz, including 10 major felonies. He was convicted of illegal weapons possession for the gun used to shoot the four teenagers. For this charge he could be sentenced to a minimum of one year in prison and a maximum of seven years, but judges are given wide discretion in sentencing, and the general feeling was that, given the wide support for Goetz, he would not even receive a minimum sentence.

Taken literally, the jurors appeared to say that it is illegal to carry an unregistered firearm, but if you happen to have one it is perfectly legal to shoot it, especially if one's victims are young Black males who may or may not rob you.

Aside from the widespread sympathy for Goetz, there were other clues indicating that he would be treated favorably by the jury. During the deliberation, one of the alternate jurors, Augustine Ayala, who sat through the deliberations but who requested to be dismissed before the verdict was announced, approached the many television cameras posted in the courthouse. He was asked by Barry Slotnick, "How are we doing?"

His reply, with a wide smile on his face was, "We're doing great." This was clearly a clue that the deliberations were favoring Goetz. In addition, six of the jurors themselves had been crime victims and were clearly convinced from the beginning that when one of the youths approached Goetz, he was reasonable in believing that this was not merely a request for money but rather the prelude to a robbery.

As has become increasingly popular, the jurors eagerly spoke with members of the press after the verdict. They reported that they never had been convinced that Goetz was guilty of anything more serious than weapons possession. They had followed Slotnick's suggestion that they discount his taped confession in which he described his actions on the subway. As if taking direct orders from Slotnick, juror James Moseley said, "The jury basically discounted the whole video-taped statement. The guy had been driving around for nine days; he'd been in the police station for twelve hours – and there were contradictions in what he said on that tape."

One juror, an airline representative, said after the trial, "There were inconsistencies in the tapes, in those confessions...I hate those tapes – they tore your heart out." Still another juror, a junior college archivist, said, "I don't believe we ever said guilty on anything else but possession of the gun he used in the subway." Although Goetz deliberately had sat down in the midst of the teenagers, one juror said it was "preposterous" to believe that Goetz "went out of his way hunting people."

One crucial piece of testimony came from Christopher Boucher, a San Francisco resident who was in the subway car when Goetz shot the four youths. Boucher testified that Darrell Cabey was sitting down when Goetz shot him. Regarding Boucher's testimony, one juror said after the trial that "It was just far-fetched. We could not find anything in the evidence that could substantially paint a theory that he could have been shot while sitting in the seat with *Bernie* Goetz standing directly in front of him." (It is of some significance that the jurors affectionately referred to Bernhard Goetz as "Bernie." Likewise, many of the local television and newspaper reports used this nickname.)

The jurors were so impressed with the subway vigilante that several of them waited in vain to have him autograph their jury service certificates. Indeed, after the jurors' verdict was rendered and they were dismissed, the *New York Times* reported that, "Several of the jurors, who were all picked up by bus at the court's rear entrance, flashed victory signs with their fingers through the bus windows." They had succeeded in contributing to the already extraordinarily high level of racial tension in New York City. Goetz look-alikes in the city were constantly harassed and chased by Black youths who were demonstrating their frustration at the racism of the criminal justice system.

THE AFTERMATH

During the 30 months between the subway shooting and the jury verdict, defenders and opponents of Goetz's behavior were very vocal in their positions. Although race was technically not an issue during the trial, undoubtedly race was the crucial issue. The jury conducted 35 separate votes over the four days of deliberations, and in none of them did anybody "cast a guilty vote on the major charges." These comments suggest that the jurors had made up their minds long before the case had ended. They, of course, denied that race played any part in the case. As one juror stated on a nationally televised news program, "My only thing I had to fall back on was the law. To suggest that this was a racial thing is just a bunch of garbage."

U.S. Attorney Guiliani announced at one point that he would consider filing federal charges against Goetz for violating the civil rights of the four teenagers, but he rejected such action because "Goetz acted out of fear – justified or not – that he would be harmed. There was no racial motivation" in the shootings. In an apparent attempt to justify the shootings just before the case went to trial, Mayor Koch wrote in a newspaper article, "We cannot avoid the fact that crime in New York City is disproportionately committed by young men who are Black." These are the young men he constantly referred to as "animals."

Although the jurors and many others maintained that the shootings were not racially motivated, most Black politicians and civil rights leaders denounced the verdict as racist. Benjamin Hooks, the former executive director of the NAACP, commented, "The jury verdict was inexcusable. I think it was a terrible and grave miscarriage of justice." He continued, "It was proven – according to his own statements – that Goetz did the shooting and went far beyond the realm of self-defense. There was no provocation for what he did." He asked, "If a White youth had been shot in similar circumstances by a Black man while the youth was prone and defenseless, what would have been the outcome then?"

Representative Floyd Flake, a Queens Democrat, said, "I think that if a Black had shot four whites, the cry for the death penalty would have been almost automatic. You won't get that in this situation."

The Black and Puerto Rican Legislative Caucus of New York State called the verdict "frightening," claiming that "it sanction[ed] dangerous vigilante actions on the part of mis-guided citizens." "Darrell Cabey's physical paralysis and Bernhard Goetz's emotional paralysis" would likely increase racial tensions in New York City the group declared.

College president and civic leader Roscoe Brown said, "The climate in which this decision was made, whether it be by White jurors or Black jurors, is one of racism and fear of young Black men."

Manhattan Borough President David Dinkins stated that he was "shaken and dismayed by the verdict," which is "a clear and open invitation to vigilantism."

The president of the New York Urban League, Harriet Michel, said the Goetz verdict "which allows people to act with less impunity on their own personal fears, is very anxiety-producing for Black people, especially for young Black men."

C. Vernon Mason, an attorney for Darrell Cabey, said that the trial had been permeated by a "racist hysteria dealing with the stereotyped image of young Black men. What we are told by this verdict is that this society cannot guarantee or assure people of African descent life or liberty – and certainly we're being frustrated at every level in the pursuit of happiness." He continued, "The common thread is color. If the 'Goetz standard' is taken to its logical conclusion, our children could become an endangered species."

Wilbert Tatum, editor of the *New York Amsterdam News*, proclaimed that the verdict represented "a tragic miscarriage of justice, not so much in terms of the young men but in terms of the fear it has engendered in all of us."

A few days after the verdict, a group of Blacks, the Disciples of Justice, organized a patrol of young Black men to protect Blacks from Goetz-type vigilantes. The group patrols the subways between 6:00pm and 6:00am. Its leaders have stated that they will intercede when they see crimes against the members of any race. One of the members, Nathaniel Cummerbath, explained why he joined the patrol: "I don't want me or my son to be picked as targets of violence or harassment because we are Black."

The furor over the subway vigilante did not subside with the verdict. Goetz's lawyers maintained after the trial that their client sought privacy. "All he wants right now is to fade into the woodwork. This has been a terrible chapter in his life – he would like to go back to being an anonymous stranger in the streets of New York." But Goetz continued to appear at pro-gun and other right-wing activities, urging citizens to arm themselves in the fight against "crime in the streets." He appeared to enjoy his celebrity status.

On April 24, 1988, he made his first public appearance in some months at the 17th anniversary celebration of the Federation of New York State Rifle and Pistol clubs. He kissed babies, sipped white wine, signed autographs, and was given a plaque for "wasting four vicious criminals and humiliating a gutless District Attorney." The 250 gun enthusiasts called him "the subway hero." With huge photographs of two of his victims near the podium, Goetz heard himself praised by the crowd. When asked if he was repentant, he said, "The judge should have sentenced me to a testimonial dinner or a ticker-tape parade." Throughout the proceedings, he wore a big smile.

Early in 1989, Goetz attended the swearing-in ceremony of members of the New York State Senate and Assembly in Albany. He was the guest of one of the new Senate members, Serphin Maltese, a Republican from Queens who had made crime-fighting the major issue in his successful campaign. Maltese said of Goetz, "Bernie's a good friend, an old friend." Said Goetz, "I'm here as an expression of support for Serph because Serph supported me publicly early on." Many people in attendance had their pictures taken with Goetz, including 8-year-old Lee Delgaudio who said to him, "Thank you for what you did for America."

When asked what Goetz had done for America, the child's father, the president of an organization that supported Colonel Oliver North in the so-called Iran-Contra case, said to him, "Remember we talked about the subway?" "Yes," he replied. "Somebody was trying to mug him and he stood up for America. Then the liberals were trying to put him in jail when he shot somebody because they were mugging him."

In an interview with a community newspaper, *Downtown Express* (December 5, 1990), Bernhard Goetz advocated a program of population control. He said, "I think that if we can control our planet we have to control our population, and I believe there should be population control policies. I think that if we don't control our population the earth will never be a decent place." He advocated both domestic population control and control of immigration. He said, "I think one of the problems in New York is that there's a problem with the lower classes reproducing at a higher rate than the rest of society and I think it's unfair." Furthermore, he advocated genetic control to make "our species better."

. . .

At the end of the trial, the judge announced that he would sentence Goetz for weapons possession at a later date. He did so on October 19, 1987. The prosecution had urged that he receive "a substantial prison sentence" because "any action by this court which unconditionally set the defendant loose in the community would, in light of his dangerous propensities, be highly irresponsible. Legitimate concern for the safety of the community demands that this court impose upon this defendant a sentence that will relieve that threat." In addition, the prosecutors maintained that Goetz "suffers from long-standing emotional disorders" and should be ordered to receive psychological treatment. The New York City Department of Probation also issued a report requesting that Goetz be ordered to undergo psychiatric treatment, but not incarceration, because he was a first-offender.

Judge Crane sentenced Goetz to six months in jail for carrying an unlicensed concealed pistol. He was also sentenced to five years probation, 280 hours of community service, ordered to undergo psychiatric counseling and fined $5,000. (Later, Goetz would be sentenced an additional 14 days because he refused to return a disposable razor to prison officials.) In pronouncing this sentence Judge Crane said, "To this court, a non-jail sentence for Mr. Goetz would invite others to violate the gun laws who, misguided or not, feel the need to arm themselves without first securing a license. Whether one agrees with the statute or not, that was the law . . . and it remains the law today."

In announcing his intention to appeal, defense attorney Slotnick said the sentence "would break New York City's heart," meaning that his client had become a sacred figure to many. No such sympathy was expressed for Darrell Cabey, who remains brain-damaged and paralyzed from the waist down as a result of the subway vigilante's fantasy. Cabey's parents, however, have sued Goetz for $50 million for his crime – although the jurors failed to see this barbaric act as a crime.

Years after Bernhard Goetz shot four Black teenagers on a New York City subway, the ramifications of the case continue. Although the shooting rendered Cabey's body permanently damaged, Goetz was acquitted of attempted murder charges. His time in jail was spent in protective custody, away from the other prisoners.

The completion of the jail term did not end Goetz's legal problems. Three of the victims filed suits totalling $63 million for injuries and punitive damages. Although Goetz inherited $140,550 from his father's estate, his legal expenses could exceed that amount. In 1988, attorney Joseph Keliner ceased to represent him when Goetz became "most uncooperative" in helping to prepare his defense and ignoring legal advice.

Acting as his own lawyer, Goetz filed a $40 million libel suit on January 9, 1990, contending that two lawyers for Darrell Cabey – William Kunstler and Ronald Kirby – called him a "walking time bomb and a racist." Cabey and his mother were also named in the suit.

9

YUSUF HAWKINS:
BENSONHURST

OVERVIEW

Ronald Reagan was no longer President in August 1989, for George Bush won the election of 1988, but Reagan-inspired anti-Black violence continued. What happened on that warm summer night of August 23 in the Bensonhurst section of Brooklyn, New York, was just another incident among many in Ronald Reagan's legacy. Reagan's contempt for the rights of Black people served to accelerate the hostile racist climate. The lynching of Yusuf Hawkins was just another act of hatred nurtured during the Reagan years. Mayor Koch, like President Reagan, contributed to the tension with his many anti-Black statements and policies.

THE ACCOUNT

According to police, 16-year-old Yusuf Hawkins and three companions (17-year-old Troy Banner, 18-year-old Claude Stanford, and 17-year-old Luther Sylvester) departed the nearby neighborhood of East New York for Bensonhurst to inspect a used car that was for sale. They had a scheduled appointment to meet with the owner of the car. When the four young men exited from the subway at around 9:00pm, they went into a candy store to buy batteries. They left the store and were later accosted by a pack of some 30 to 40 white youths armed with baseball bats, hand guns, knives, and other weapons. Words were exchanged between Hawkins and his friends and the gang of white youths. Witnesses reported they had overheard this exchange from the gang of whites: "Let's club the niggers," said one. "No, let's not club, let's shoot one," said another.

Suddenly, four shots were fired, and young Hawkins caught two in the chest. Troy Banner suffered a graze wound but was not seriously injured. Claude Stanford and Luther Sylvester escaped injury. A resident who heard the shots rushed to the scene and found Hawkins on the ground clutching a candy bar. This is how Elizabeth Galarza, 32, a neighborhood resident, described the scene: "His pulse was still there – it was pretty good on his neck. He was blinking his eyes. He couldn't talk. I pulled up his T-shirt. I saw two bullet holes in his chest." She continued, "The young boy clenched my hand. When his pulse stopped, he clenched tight and let go. He was frightened. He had terror in his eyes. He was so young and so frightened.

I said, 'Come on baby. You'll be fine. Take small breaths. God's with you.'" Galarza said she then called the police, who arrived 15 minutes later. Yusuf Hawkins was dead on arrival at Maimonides Medical Center.

The police arrested 18-year-old Steven Curreri, 18-year-old Keith Mondello, 18-year-old-Brian O'Donnel, and 19-year-old Pasquale Raucci. The police reported that a Bensonhurst girl, 18-year-old Gina Feliciano, was going to celebrate her birthday that night with a party to which she invited Black and Puerto Rican friends, but had cancelled the party when she heard that the white youths were planning to cause trouble. Feliciano told Mondello, a suitor whom she had spurned, that she had invited as many as 30 Black and Puerto Rican youths to the party. Mondello reportedly had become agitated when he heard that she had dated Black and Hispanic men. (Although there are few Puerto Ricans in the neighborhood, Feliciano noted that her father, who had been killed in Vietnam, was Puerto Rican.) Feliciano told the police that minutes before the shooting, a member of the white gang showed her a gun and told her, "You better watch yourself with your nigger friends." They then gathered outside the building in which she lived, waiting for her friends to arrive. It was there that Yusuf Hawkins was killed.

The following day, the police arrested two more suspects – James Patino, 24, and Charles Stressler, 21. Like the other four who had been arrested, they were charged with both felonies and misdemeanors, including aggravated assault, riot, conspiracy, violation of civil rights, and menacing.

In the meantime, the police began an intensive search for another white youth, Joseph Fama, 18, who some witnesses claimed was the gunman in the attack. Fama was described as a high school dropout who worked with his father at a neighborhood construction company and who enjoyed taking hunting trips with his father to the Catskill Mountains. Both of Fama's parents were Italian immigrants, and because he had been born in New York, he held dual American and Italian citizenship.

An organization of community leaders formed after the Howard Beach attack that left Michael Griffith dead – the New York City Civil Rights Coalition – met to discuss the death of Yusuf Hawkins at the offices of the American Civil Liberties Union. Galen Kirland, the executive director of the Coalition said, "New York is a racially segregated city in desperate trouble. It is a city where you can be killed for taking a wrong turn because of racial violence."

With few exceptions, residents of Bensonhurst showed little sympathy for the murdered Black teenager. They expressed solidarity with those being held for the crime, condemned the media for its widespread reporting of the case, and questioned why the Black teenagers were in the neighborhood. One resident, Michael Campanelli, 18, asked, "Why was he buying a car at 16? What does he know about cars?" Still another asked, "Why would someone come down at nine o'clock to buy a car?" These two comments expressed the general community view that Blacks should not have been in Bensonhurst. One unidentified resident, in defense of the right of all citizens to walk the streets of all neighborhoods without fear, said, "A 16-year-old boy should be allowed to go where he wants to go. There is such a thing as off limits. This is not Russia." The mother of Pasquale Raucci, one of the suspects, expressed her sympathy for the victim's family, saying, "I am not feeling half as bad as the poor boy's mother."

The killing of Yusuf Hawkins took place as the mayoral primary race in New York City was in high gear. It was, therefore, destined to become a part of the campaign, although all candidates had expressed the hope that it would not be exploited for political purposes. Both a leading Democratic candidate, David Dinkins, Manhattan Borough President and the only Black candidate in the race, and Rudolph Guiliani, the former federal prosecutor and Republican candidate, issued statements saying that the political climate created by Mayor Koch was partly responsible for the racial violence. After expressing his outrage at the killing, Dinkins said, "I certainly do not wish to accuse the Mayor or anyone else of causing this. But let me say that the tone and climate of this city does get set at City Hall." Guiliani's statement was even harsher: "The incident speaks volumes about the racial tensions in our city, tensions which are fueled by a mayor who divides rather than deals and who governs by name calling, bringing out the worst in us, rather than the best."

Blacks and politicians were not the only ones who condemned the Mayor's comments and actions. *New York Times* columnist Anthony Lewis wrote of Koch's role in exacerbating racial tensions: "...in New York City the vacuum of leadership has been especially painful. The Mayor, Edward Koch, has made clear by dozens of actions over the years that he does not care about Blacks."

When large groups of Black and white demonstrators protested the lynching with a march through the streets of Bensonhurst, Mayor Koch reacted by opposing the demonstrations, although he did not challenge the people's right to protest anywhere in the city. "The question is: Do you want to be helpful to reduce the tensions or do you want to escalate the tensions?" he asked. "It's just as wrong to march into Bensonhurst as it would be to march in Harlem after that young woman in the jogging case." He was referring to charges brought against six Black and Puerto Rican teenagers from East Harlem charged with the rape and assault of a white investment banker in Central Park the preceding April. This position was no doubt taken because the Mayor had depended on blue-collar white voters like those in Bensonhurst in past elections and was careful not to alienate this crucial component of his constituency. Inasmuch as Bensonhurst residents had protested the marches, Koch's statement served as an appeal for votes in the upcoming election.

Regarding Koch's comments, an official of the American Civil Liberties Union wrote: "[Koch] did not urge the good people to come out. Instead, like his southern predecessors a generation ago, he asked the protestors to go back where they came from. He resurrected the old 'outside agitator' theory of unrest once so popular with southern elected officials and a perennial favorite of establishments around the globe whenever the winds of change begin to blow." He continued, "Now comes Mayor Koch to instruct that those who hailed from parts outside of Bensonhurst were only exacerbating racial tensions by staking their equal claim to all the streets of New York."

Dinkins took issue with the Mayor, stating that the demonstrations were in "the finest tradition in our country. To suggest that peaceful demonstrations led by members of the clergy, had no right to be there, that somehow would exacerbate tension is a position from which I dissent." Guiliani noted that the Mayor's comments had served the function of "politicizing this unfortunate incident." And another Democratic candidate, Richard Ravitch, said he thought the peaceful protests were appropriate.

On the Saturday following the murder, the first of several protest demonstrations and marches was held in Bensonhurst. They were lead by a coalition of ministers and civic leaders. But when they reached this largely Italian American community, they found that there was little, if any, remorse or sympathy in Bensonhurst. Hundreds of whites, largely teenage males, some wearing Ku Klux Klan t-shirts, greeted the marchers with racial epithets and threats of violence. Chanting "Niggers go home" at the largely Black group of demonstrators, many held watermelons in the air and carried signs with obscene slogans. Some carried signs in praise of South Africa's policy of racial segregation, and some carried placards with Nazi symbols on them.

191

During these demonstrations, several scuffles broke out, but there was no violence because of the hundreds of police on patrol. The demonstrations were among the most racist in the memory of most people. (The true nature of the demonstrators was not lost on most people when they saw young men holding watermelons in the air next to one carrying a sign proclaiming "We are not racists.") Rarely had such demonstrations in the southern states brought forth such racist and angry remarks. As one of the marchers said, "You couldn't get any uglier scene than this in Mississippi." It is not difficult to imagine that many of the marchers would have been killed, again without remorse, if the police had not been out in such large numbers. If there were remorseful residents in this close-knit, insular community, they did not come out to support the marchers or condemn the racist tactics. Yet, residents repeatedly complained that the media presented the wrong image of Bensonhurst. It was as if news programs had rerun tapes of the 1986 Howard Beach demonstrations. The crowds of whites clearly resembled a wild mob; they appeared eager to show the world the depth of their racism.

On the next day, two additional demonstrations were held in Brooklyn. One demonstration, led by clergymen from throughout the city, met at the site of the murder and marched five blocks to St. Dominic's Roman Catholic Church, where a rally was held. This demonstration, which was called a "service of reclamation and possession of the city," was also met with screams of obscenities and racial slurs from hundreds of local residents. They demanded that the arrested youths ("the boys from Bensonhurst") be released and that the demonstrators "go home."

Commenting on the racist counter-demonstrations, the *New York Times,* in an editorial entitled "Racism, Accomplice to Murder," had this to say: "Anyone who thought the murder of Yusuf Hawkins in the Bensonhurst section of Brooklyn was an isolated incident had to wait only three days to learn differently. When scores of mourners, led by ministers, paraded in the streets Sunday to express their outrage, they were confronted by a crowd so angry and insulting it had to be restrained behind police barriers."

Meanwhile, local ministers could not avoid involvement in events in Bensonhurst, a largely Roman Catholic community. Bishop Francis J. Mugavero of the Catholic Diocese of Brooklyn stated that the demonstrations might have inflamed racist tensions and unfairly blamed the community for the actions of a few. "You have to wonder what was accomplished by going into a community" to protest, he said. But Reverend Charles S. Fermeglia of St. Dominic's Church opened his 9:30am mass by comparing the murdered Yusuf Hawkins to Jesus Christ – "another innocent man who was misunderstood." "Sometimes," he said, "our religion does not reflect the way we live." Several parishioners came to the clergyman with tears in their eyes. Said Carmella Collandria, "A child died, and a mother is in pain. That's the way I feel." At the same time, on the same street, hundreds of teenagers, waving Italian and American flags, were taunting and jeering marchers. Commenting on the insularity of Bensonhurst, the priest said in an interview, "This is a very provincial community. A lot of these kids don't know what life is outside of Bensonhurst. Heck, some of the boys on 20th Avenue don't even know what life is like on 13th Avenue."

A week after the killing, six more youths were arrested, but the prime suspect, Joseph Fama, had eluded the police, including 50 special detectives who searched the community for him. The youngest of three children whose parents, Josephine and Rocco Fama, emigrated from Calabria, Italy before he was born, Fama grew up in Bensonhurst — a few blocks from the site of the murder.

The August 29th wake for Yusuf Hawkins drew thousands of mourners to the funeral home, including Reverend Jesse Jackson, a two-time candidate for the Democratic nomination for president. Jackson told the hundreds of mourners, "We will stand with the family. We will stand tall in the midst of this madness. The whole nation must have a sense of outrage." When Mayor Koch arrived, the crowd shouted, "No! No!" A cousin of Yusuf Hawkins, Betty Jones, ran to the door of the chapel in an attempt to bar the Mayor's entry. She said, "My cousin is not a political thing." But Moses Stewart, the dead boy's father, led Koch to the coffin. Later, Stewart told reporters, "I'm not endorsing Koch, I'm not endorsing Dinkins. I just don't want anyone here being disrespectful over my son."

As the mourners walked past the coffin, some of them expressed their grief openly. Said one elderly woman, "I can't stand it. It hurts so much." Another said, "I'm here as a mother. I heard about it. I have nephews his age. I just wanted to sympathize with them." Still another said, "I'm a little angry....He didn't deserve to die this way." And Jeanette Matthews said, "The North is becoming the South, and the South is becoming the North. It's getting ridiculous. We need a passport to go to some parts of Brooklyn." She continued, "I'm angry, I'm hurt, I'm afraid. My grandparents went through this. My parents went through this. Do my children have to go through this too?"

The funeral was held the following day and was used by many speakers not only to reflect on Yusuf Hawkins but to comment on the heightened racial tensions in New York City. The funeral was attended by thousands, but only some 300 people were permitted inside Glover Memorial Baptist Church. Among those in attendance were Reverend Jesse Jackson, Governor Mario Cuomo, Mayor Edward Koch, Minister Louis Farrakhan (who also provided security guards for the funeral) and four of the six candidates for mayor.

As a demonstration of the low esteem in which New York politicians are held, the candidates were required to stand outside in the crowd, listening to hecklers, for an hour before being permitted to enter the church. Once inside, they heard many speakers comment on the state of race relations in New York, some of whom directed their remarks directly to them. For example, Reverend Curtis Wells, the minister of Glover Memorial and a relative of the murdered youth, said, "Mr.

Mayor, Mr. Governor, let freedom ring in Howard Beach. Let freedom ring in Wappingers Falls [the hometown of Tawana Brawley, the teenager who claimed that she had been abducted and raped by a group of white men]. Let freedom ring, yes, in Bensonhurst."

On August 31, Joseph Fama walked into the police station in the small town of Oneonta, New York, said he was wanted for murder in New York City, and turned himself in. According to the police in this town of 15,000 residents some 180 miles northwest of New York City, Fama claimed that he had hitchhiked to Oneonta and had been roaming the streets. Insisting that he was innocent of the murder, he said he surrendered because he was "tired of being accused of something" he did not do. He expressed concern for his family, especially his mother, and said he had not called home because he feared that the telephones were tapped. Fama was returned to New York City the following day, where he pleaded not guilty to two counts of second-degree murder and other charges.

Meanwhile, protests continued, including a massive demonstration by a group police estimated at 8,000, on what was called the "Day of Outrage and Mourning." This theme had been used in past years to protest the murders of Eleanor Bumpers, Michael Stewart, and Michael Griffith; but this was the largest demonstration of its kind, and the police did not expect so many people. The demonstrators gathered to protest the murder of Yusuf Hawkins and that of Huey P. Newton, the co-founder of the Black Panther Party, who was killed in Oakland, California, on August 22.

The protestors gathered at Grand Army Plaza in Brooklyn and marched through the borough's downtown section to the Brooklyn Bridge. Inasmuch as the demonstration was planned to coincide with the rush hour, the traffic in downtown Brooklyn was disrupted. When the demonstrators, who formed a line that stretched for 20 blocks, reached the bridge, they decided to cross it, which had not been part of the original plan. They clashed with police, who attempted to prevent them from crossing. During the melee, demonstrators hurled bottles, bricks, and other missiles, wounding at least 44 police officers, including David W. Scott, the officer in charge and the police department's Chief of Patrol. Four civilians, including two photographers, were arrested. The demonstration lasted four hours. Representatives of dozens of activist organizations and others joined the confrontation, which was organized by the December 12 Movement, an organization formed to protest anti-Black violence.

The following day, some 300 demonstrators marched through Bensonhurst. The marchers were flanked by a force of 400 police officers. As usual, these peaceful demonstrators, who carried Black liberation flags, were met by mobs of white residents who shouted obscenities and racial epithets such as "Niggers, go home," "You Savages" and "Long Live South Africa." Referring to Yusuf Hawkins and his companions, 22-year-old Joseph Bono commented, "We don't go to Harlem. The kids were in the wrong spot." "This is Bensonhurst," he declared, "It is all Italian. We don't need these niggers." Added another resident, Michael Fenga, "No one likes no one if they don't look the same. Everybody's prejudiced. And that's the way it is."

As the marchers chanted "Animals! Animals!," one resident said, "It's a disgrace. We're being labeled animals and we're decent people." Another said, "If we were animals, we wouldn't let them into our neighborhood."

On the other hand, "the good people" of Bensonhurst, a group of 200 residents, met for mass and a march through the neighborhood on September 3. During the mass, priests at St. Dominic's Roman Catholic Church offered prayers for "the repose of the soul of Yusuf Hawkins." The associate pastor of the church, Reverend Al Barozzi, led the mass, which was given in Italian. He said, "Walking silently and praying in our hearts can be as powerful as protests and shouting and maybe even killing." After the mass, which was joined by priests from several other Bensonhurst parishes, the worshippers, who were joined by others, marched from the church to the site where Hawkins had been murdered. There, a wreath of roses and carnations were placed and the Lord's Prayer was recited. In the brief religious ceremony at the cite, Reverend Arthur G. Minichello declared, "Lord, let the death of this young man be a sign that two communities, Black and White, can learn to love one another."

As lawyers for the defendants prepared to go to trial, they maintained that the attack was not racially motivated. Rather, they claimed that the shooting was a tragic mistake, that their clients thought they were going to be accosted by a gang of Blacks and Hispanics (friends of Gina Feliciano), and that she, Feliciano, was responsible for the incident. Feliciano, they said, had threatened to have her Black and Hispanic friends come to the neighborhood to attack the neighborhood residents. She had, in their opinion, violated the mores of the neighborhood by dating Black and Hispanic men. They also pointed out that one of the accused, Charles Stressler, was the best friend of a young Black man, Russell Gibbons. The defense lawyers also pointed out that Gibbons regularly spent time with those accused in the case and that he had assisted in collecting the baseball bats used in the attack. They argued that if white youths had threatened to come to a Black community to fight, the residents also would have protected themselves.

In the meantime, Gina Feliciano said that because of death threats she had received, she would go into hiding with police protection. In addition, she said that there was a $100,000 contract put out by somebody who wanted her killed. She was interviewed on the CBS news program *60 Minutes* on October 15, from a hotel room in an undisclosed location. When asked why she had more Black and Hispanic friends than Italian she said, "Those are the people I feel comfortable around." Asked if she would testify against the Bensonhurst residents accused in this case, she replied, "You gotta take a stand once in your life. And right now I feel that this is my stand."

All the defendants in the case, except Joseph Fama, were released on bail ranging from $75,000 to $100,000. This caused some controversy because, at about the same time, the six Blacks and Hispanics arrested in the assault and rape of a white female banker in Central Park were initially denied bail, and no one was killed in that incident. And unlike the Bensonhurst defendants, only one of whom was initially charged with murder, all of the Central Park defendants were initially charged with attempted murder. Furthermore, all of the defendants in the Central Park case had significant community ties, decreasing the likelihood that they would flee. This caused many people to question whether justice in New York City was indeed colorblind.

THE PERPETRATORS

The eight defendants ultimately charged in the case were all from the Bensonhurst area:

Steven Curreri, 18, a graduate of Franklin D. Roosevelt High School and a student at Kingsborough Junior College, was charged with first-degree assault, riot, and criminal possession of a weapon.

Joseph Fama, 18, attended public schools in the neighborhood, graduating from Edward B. Shallow Junior High School. He attended New Utrecht High School but dropped out after one year. Fama was charged with two counts of second-degree murder, first-degree assault, riot, criminal possession of a weapon, and conspiracy.

Keith Mondello, 18, a construction supervisor at a local firm, was charged with murder, manslaughter, first-degree riot, aggravated assault, unlawful imprisonment, and several misdemeanors.

James Patino, 24, graduated from New Utrecht High School and Staten Island Community College. At the time of his arrest, he was unemployed. Patino was charged with murder, manslaughter, riot, and discrimination.

Pasquale Raucci, 19, was an employee of a video store at the time of his arrest. He was charged with second-degree murder, first- and second-degree manslaughter, assault, first-degree riot, aggravated assault, harassment, and two misdemeanors.

Joseph Serrano, 19, was identified by one witness as one of the persons with a gun, but it was said that he did not fire it. Serrano was charged with assault, riot, aggravated harassment, civil rights violation, and menacing.

Charles Stressler, 21, a student at Kings Borough Community College, was working as a carpenter's apprentice at the time of his arrest. He was charged with second-degree murder, first-degree riot, aggravated harassment, criminal possession of a weapon, and violation of civil rights.

John S. Vento, 21, originally agreed to testify for the prosecution in exchange for having his most serious charges dropped. When he later refused to cooperate, he was charged with second-degree murder, manslaughter, riot, and several misdemeanors.

THE VICTIM

Yusuf Hawkins lived with his parents, Diane Hawkins and Moses Stewart, in the East New York section of Brooklyn. The neighborhood in which they lived is not unlike that of those accused in his death: it is a community of home owners, many of whom are construction workers or civil servants. These blue-collar workers, most of whom are immigrants from the Caribbean, live in renovated houses with neat gardens.

Hawkins was remembered by neighbors as an outgoing and friendly teenager who often ran errands for the older people in the community, where his grandmother also lived. He enjoyed playing basketball and going to movies. In a radio interview his father described him as "very, very intelligent" and said he had been accepted at a technical high school. He said his son had already received many certificates and diplomas. "He was reaching his goals," Stewart said. "He was putting his dreams behind him because he was achieving his task."

PROFILE: BENSONHURST

What kind of community is Bensonhurst? Watching television news programs or reading newspaper accounts of the murder of Yusuf Hawkins, or even the accounts of residents during the trials of those accused of his death, one imagines this Brooklyn community to be an exaggeration of the most racist and violent of places, even worse than the South during the civil rights demonstrations — worse than South Africa at its worst. It is a closed, working-class neighborhood, consisting largely of immigrants from Italy and their descendants. Nearly half of its 153,000 residents are recent immigrants, mostly from Sicily and southern Italy. One is likely to hear Italian spoken as often as English.

Probably the most characteristic feature of this community is its insularity. It exists as though it is not part of New York City, with its residents fiercely and often violently guarding their territory. Unlike much of New York City, it has changed little through the years. There are few, if any, Blacks, Asians, or Hispanics in Bensonhurst.

Bensonhurst is a neighborhood of two- and three-family houses, with well-kept yards and religious statues. During the Christmas season, the homes are heavily decorated with lights and other paraphernalia. During patriotic holidays, the community is full of American and Italian flags. The shopping streets are lined with Italian pasta and pastry shops and pork stores. There are also several social clubs, usually named after places in Italy, where old men drink espresso coffee while playing cards.

In the evenings, young men gather on street corners or at candy stores to drink beer. Bensonhurst is a world of tightly-knit families, where members interact only with each other and where outsiders are feared and resented. Often, residents refer to the community as their extended family. A local priest said of his parishioners, "They are trying to transplant the same ties they had in Italy, their food, their relationships, the people they gossip with, because it gives meaning to their lives."

LEST WE FORGET: WHITE HATE CRIMES

One of the biggest community events of the year is the Feast of Santa Rosalia. The streets are covered with red, white, and green banners and lights, representing the colors of the Italian flag. Speaking of Santa Rosalia, Joseph Galatolo, the chairman of the feast committee, said, "She performed a lot of miracles at a very young age and died when she was fourteen. Her father was a prince, but she didn't want to marry royalty. She wanted to be with the people, so she went into the grotto and died. Because of the miracles, people left their jewelry there."

Because of the killing of Yusuf Hawkins and the protest demonstrations that followed, the feast was not as well attended in 1989 as in previous years. Speaking of the largely Black demonstrators, one 13-year-old exclaimed, "They are just ruining the feast. Nobody is allowed to go off the block. They're ruining the reputation of Bensonhurst."

The insular character of Bensonhurst, with its fear of outsiders, contributes to the negative feelings so many of its residents hold about nonwhite minorities. And while they proclaim their lack of racial prejudice, other incidents that occurred during the Reagan/Koch era illustrate why residents of this community have earned a reputation for racial intolerance. In 1983, three Black men who were on their way home from work at a nearby hospital were beaten by a group of whites in Bensonhurst. In 1987, two Black men, who were collecting redeemable bottles and cans, were beaten by a group of white Bensonhurst residents. Shouting racial epithets at the Black men, they chased them and beat them with sticks, a marble slab, and a knife.

Shortly after the racial attack in Howard Beach, 20-year-old Samuel Spencer III was murdered in the Coney Island section of Brooklyn by four residents of nearby Bensonhurst. On the afternoon of May 27, 1986, Spencer left the apartment he shared with his sister in a building managed by their father. He said he was going to a restaurant, but he never returned. While riding his bicycle early the next morning on Surf Avenue near Nathan's restaurant, he encountered a group of young men leaning on parked cars. Exactly what happened is difficult to ascertain; the police said his bicycle clashed with one of the automobiles and a shouting match ensued. Spencer fled but was pursued by the young white men in cars. One of the cars drove onto the sidewalk and cut him off. He fell from his bicycle and was brutally beaten by the mob. He was pronounced dead at Coney Island Hospital at around 4:00am on May 28, 1986. He had been beaten with a baseball bat and stabbed three times in the back.

Several weeks later, three men – Frank Casavilla, 19, Frank D'Antonio, 23, and Cosmo Muriale, 26 – were arrested in their Bensonhurst homes and charged with second-degree murder and possession of deadly weapons. Another defendant in the case, Douglas Mackay, was arrested later. Casavella pleaded guilty to second-degree murder on January 25, 1988, just before the beginning of opening arguments in the trial. He reported that as he stabbed Spencer, he said, "You're going to die now, nigger." When asked why he entered the guilty plea, he replied that since the Howard Beach case, he thought he would have received a longer sentence. Mackay pleaded guilty on January 21, but D'Antonio and Muriale pleaded not guilty.

Lamenting the dearth of publicity her son's murder received, Tina Spencer, a bookkeeper for an advertising agency, later told a reporter that "If they had given my son's case recognition maybe the Griffith boy would be here and maybe Yusuf would be here."

Bensonhurst is usually described by residents as a peaceful, law-abiding community of well-maintained houses on tree-lined streets. The impression is conveyed that this is an ideal lower- to middle-class neighborhood. However, two reporters from the *Village Voice*, Mark Bauman and Samme Chittum, spent months studying Bensonhurst before the Hawkins murder, and they reported a different picture. They wrote, "The violence that underlies the neighborhood's calm surface is revealed in small as well as dramatic ways. Even when the guys on the corner are not doing anything that might attract police attention, they play at being wise guys." They added that, "Most of them own BB guns. And on a really slow night they meander down to Gravesend Bay to shoot rats – 'target practice' – for more serious games." According to these reporters, casual violence is widespread among the young men who hang out on street corners. A regular on the street corners described for them how he was shot by another street-corner regular: "That cocksucker shot me in the ass. That was a real professional hit." He then related how the acquaintance pulled up in his car, rolled down the window, and shot him several times.

He then said, "That's all right. I'll get him later." Commenting on the insular character of Bensonhurst, these reporters wrote, "Breaking the neighborhood rules is not tolerated, but breaking the law is, especially if it involves crime in a minority neighborhood." They quoted a resident who worked as bodyguard for a drug dealer in a nearby Puerto Rican community. He said, "They're all punks over there. It ain't nothin'. I mean if we wanted to go over there and start takin' over, it would be no problem."

Regarding the socialization of children in Bensonhurst, Bauman and Chittum reported that "From an early age, Bensonhurst kids are taught to look the other way when questionable business in progress involves their own. Dishonesty isn't a crime, but giving up the wrong people is." One resident told them this childhood experience: "A guy my father knew walked out of his house. My father said, 'where's Tony?' I said, 'Right over there.' He smacked me. 'You don't see nothing,' he said, 'You never see Tony.'" This attitude of secrecy helps to explain the "communal amnesia" displayed by the residents who watched the murder of Yusuf Hawkins but refused to admit that they saw anything.

As with the Howard Beach community, it has been rumored that organized crime thrives in Bensonhurst. the *New York Times* reported that "Federal prosecutors say the Mafia also has a strong presence in the community, although most people are reluctant to mention its activities." One defendant in the Hawkins case, John Vento, initially agreed to cooperate with the prosecution in exchange for a reduction in charges, but he later reneged on the agreement because threats had been made to his family. His attorney insisted that the threats had come from organized crime.

According to the reporters from the *Village Voice*, Bensonhurst is a community with a strong Mafia tradition. "Seldom discussed except in oblique references, the Mafia presence still pervades Bensonhurst, cloaking the neighborhood in ostentatious secrecy, like the tinted windows of the stretch limousines that line 18th Avenue." They continued "Although only lower-level Mafiosa still live [t]here, the big players do business in the small but exclusive cafes that line 18th Avenue." One detective described to them the reverence with which organized crime figures are held. "These guys are heroes to the kids," he said. A local resident said that if one annoyed the wrong people, difficulty was likely to follow "cause they'll shoot you in the head and not think about it the next day." A local priest reported that his parish had recently buried two young men, whom he assumed were "killed by the mob."

The young men who hang out on the corners in the neighborhood see Bensonhurst as "the last Italian neighborhood" in New York, and they are determined to keep it that way. What many consider to be simply a close-knit community struggling to survive in the midst of change, others see as a dangerous community that is armed and determined to retain its "ethnic purity." Of course, social change is frequently resisted elsewhere, but rarely with such fervor as has been witnessed in

Bensonhurst. The young men of this community are "fortified by their faith in the Godfather myth and armed with baseball bats, beer bottles, and pamphlets calling for a boycott of local Chinese businesses, the youth of Bensonhurst have taken their battle to the streets," noted the *Village Voice*. " 'This neighborhood has been Italian for 100 years and it's not going to change,' vows Salina Reyna, a neighborhood loyalist."

Although it was frequently said that the racist residents in Bensonhurst did not represent the community, it is unlikely that much resistance to this behavior existed because of what has been called the "culture of racism" that pervades the community. This is a culture that "privately permits and encourages racist attitudes and fears, that allows the word 'nigger' to be used at the dinner table in 'decent' homes; that permits young people to be taught to hate and fear the 'other' and to judge people . . . by their skin color, religion, or sexual orientation," so wrote Ira Glasser, an official of the ACLU. Glasser noted that, "The cultural tolerance of racism by the good people of Birmingham, Alabama, and their steadfast silence in the face of racial violence, nourished the lunatics who one day blew up four little Black girls in a local church." He concluded, "What must trouble us, finally, about the young men who murdered Yusuf Hawkins is not that they are an aberration, but that they are *typical*; they are *normal*, they *reflect* the neighborhood far more than they deviate from it." It is clearly unlikely that such intensely held racist attitudes as the residents displayed could have existed if they had not been learned during childhood.

Based on the picture presented to the world by the residents of Bensonhurst themselves, this culture of racism was accurately depicted by Spike Lee in his movie *Jungle Fever*. A Black woman, Leona Nichols, who has worked in the post office in Bensonhurst for more than 20 years, said she has never felt welcome in the community. She confided that she has had her share of problems there: "People look at you as if you don't belong here." Residents have frequently told her, "Nigger, you don't belong here," she said. "I've learned to get into my car after work and leave." It is also unlikely that such attitudes would not have been transformed into such violent behavior without the support given them by leaders in Washington and New York City.

While the murder of Yusuf Hawkins was motivated by the racism so widespread in Bensonhurst, some economic factors no doubt played a role or at least served to intensify existing racism. Schools in the community have high dropout rates, and unemployment is common. As a local priest pointed out, many of the residents are recent immigrants who "come to America because there's no possibility of getting jobs in Italy, and the jobs they get here, mostly blue-collar jobs, are gotten through relatives."

Many of the young men depend on the construction industry or civil service employment, but such jobs are few in a period of recession. Furthermore, because of affirmative action legislation, they must compete with Blacks and other minorities for existing jobs, and often minorities have more formal education. Many of the young men in Bensonhurst claim they no longer apply for public service jobs because they assume they are reserved for Blacks. They blame affirmative action for their economic plight, and since minorities and women are seen as its beneficiaries, these groups (especially people of color) are the objects of their frustration.

Bensonhurst and some other ethnic enclaves formed when second- and third- generation families of European immigrants moved from Brooklyn neighborhoods like Park Slope and Carroll Gardens during the last few decades in order to distance themselves from Blacks and Hispanics. They sought places like Bensonhurst and Howard Beach because they believed their former neighborhoods were being "invaded." And working-class neighborhoods generally cling to society's harshest stereotypes of minorities.

A former Bensonhurst resident, who left the community to go to college and did not return, recalled that when he was growing up there he was afraid of the angry young men who hung out on street corners and in front of candy stores drinking beer and fighting. He said he was afraid he might become one of them. Frank Pugliese's play, *Aven' U Boys*, which opened in New York after the murder of Yusuf Hawkins but before the trial, is set in Bensonhurst. He said the title refers to a street in the community where young men gather. The plot of the play centers on the fatal beating of a Black man who, in search of a place to purchase a sandwich, enters the neighborhood and is accosted by three white youths who beat him to death. Pugliese said he wrote the play seven years earlier during his second year

211

at Cornell University. Two weeks after it went into rehearsals, Yusuf Hawkins was killed. He said that the killing of Hawkins did not surprise him because Bensonhurst is a neighborhood where many of the young men are so full of racial hatred that they are capable of murder.

THE TRIALS

The trials of Joseph Fama and Keith Mondello were scheduled to begin on March 5, 1990. Judge Thaddeus Owens ordered separate trials for Fama and Mondello. The trials were to be conducted at the same time in the same courtroom before the same judge, but two juries were required because some of the prosecution's evidence could not be used against both defendants. Also, one trial, rather than two, is less expensive and more efficient. Before it could begin, however, John Vento, who participated in the attack but who agreed to testify for the prosecution in exchange for having charges against him reduced, disappeared. His disappearance forced a delay, and the trial was rescheduled for April 2.

After two months, Vento turned himself in to federal officials in Dayton, Ohio, on March 5. He reported that during his absence he had lived with his brother, Michael Vento, in Liverpool, New York, near Syracuse. After his return to New York City, he informed the District Attorney that he would not keep his pledge to testify; he was immediately charged with second-degree murder and other offenses.

This action was but one of several setbacks for the prosecution. Earlier, Gina Feliciano, the principle witness for the prosecution, entered a drug treatment program. One of the defense lawyers, Bruce McIntire, who is Black, resigned from the case charging that he was being used as a token. Two witnesses who claimed that Fama had confessed to the murder while in jail with them were described as confidence men who were serving lengthy sentences for serious crimes; thus, their testimony could not be relied on. Finally, Russell Gibbons, the Black man who was friendly with several of the accused, agreed to testify that he collected the baseball bats used in the killing, thereby possibly weakening the prosecution's charge that the attack was racial.

Nevertheless, jury selection for the trials of Fama and Mondello commenced on April 12. Fama's jury consisted of three Blacks, six whites, two Hispanics, and one Native American. Mondello's had three Blacks, three Hispanics, and six whites. Each jury heard the same evidence.

In a videotaped interview played at the trial, Mondello admitted to the police that he and a group of white friends had gathered the night of the murder, but he said, "We wanted to protect ourselves." He said that Gina Feliciano had told him that a group of Blacks and Hispanics was coming to "beat up" him and his friends. The prosecution called an inmate, Charles Brown, to testify. He said that he had been in prison since 1974, except for a few months, and that he had a long list of criminal offenses. Brown said that while in the Brooklyn House of

Detention he had met Fama, who confessed to killing Hawkins. A second prisoner with a long criminal career, Robert Russo, said that Fama had told him in jail that he had killed Hawkins because he was "a nigger."

The mother of Gina Feliciano, Phyllis D'Agata, who lived on the second floor above the site where Hawkins was killed, testified that she had heard Mondello say to Joseph Serrano, "Let's club the niggers." To this Serrano is said to have replied, "Let's not club the niggers, let's shoot them and show Gina."

The only Bensonhurst resident to testify that he saw Fama shoot Hawkins was Franklin Tighe, who had been treated for mental disorders and who admitted to having hallucinations. All of the other residents of the community either testified that they did not see anything or could not recall what they saw. There were dozens of local residents present when Hawkins was killed, but they refused to cooperate with the prosecution. This "communal amnesia," as one reporter called the inability of Bensonhurst residents to remember, would ultimately serve to weaken the prosecution's case.

The jury in the Fama case rendered its verdict on May 17, and the Mondello jury rendered its verdict on May 18. Fama was found guilty of second-degree murder "with depraved indifference for human life" and 13 other charges, including first-degree riot, three counts of first-degree unlawful imprisonment, and three counts of menacing. The members of the jury said they were convinced that Fama was part of the mob that killed Hawkins, but were not sure that he fired the fatal shots. Thus, they were unable to convict him of intentional murder.

Keith Mondello was acquitted of four counts of murder and manslaughter the following day, although his jury heard the same evidence as Fama's jury. Mondello was convicted of the lesser charges of first-degree riot, three counts of first-degree unlawful imprisonment, three counts of menacing, four counts of discrimination, and fourth-degree criminal possession of a weapon. Jurors in this case said they based their decision on the evidence presented to them. They said the verdict had been a compromise. One juror reported later that most jurors initially favored convicting Mondello of manslaughter, but two of them, both white, said they "wouldn't convict Mondello in no way, form or fashion."

Mondello's case was considered to be more important than Fama's. Mondello had confessed in the videotaped interview with police that he had carried a baseball bat and that he was among those who had surrounded Hawkins. He later claimed that his confession had been coerced by police.

Upon hearing the Fama verdict, many of Hawkins' supporters who had attended the trial remained calm, but when the Mondello verdict was announced, demonstrators gathered in downtown Brooklyn and marched to Hawkins' home, knocking over garbage cans as they proceeded. But there was no major violence. In Bensonhurst, on the other hand, people celebrated in the streets.

LEST WE FORGET: WHITE HATE CRIMES

When the jury in the Mondello case announced its verdict, there were angry outbursts in the courtroom. Some spectators cried, "He did it! He did it!" One of them attempted to reach the defendant's father, who was sitting nearby, but he was restrained by court officers. One spectator shouted "We'll do it ourselves!" Outside the courthouse, a crowd had gathered. They chanted "Burn Bensonhurst" as they burned an American flag.

The following day, a group of some 600 persons, most of them Black, arrived in Bensonhurst to demonstrate their anger with the Mondello verdict. They were led by Reverend Al Sharpton, who served as spokesperson for the Hawkins family. When they started to march, they were met by a mob of whites who were noisier and more outspoken in their anti-Black feelings than those who had gathered in earlier protests. As usual they shouted racial epithets and obscenities at the marchers. Some of the mob held up watermelons, while others twirled basketballs on their fingertips. In an expression of solidarity with Joseph Fama, they yelled, "Joey, Joey, Joey." They yelled to the marchers, "Nigger, nigger!" One white heckler shouted, "You're all a bunch of crack heads." Andrea Porter, a 53-year-old nurse who walked among the marchers, said, "I can't believe this. Nothing has changed. They are treating us the same way they did a year ago when we first marched here. These people are inhuman."

The depth of racial hatred demonstrated by the residents of Bensonhurst throughout the months following the murder and during the trials was so intense that one civil libertarian wrote that the marchers were "greeted by those snarling faces, as if the dead memories of Little Rock had been satanically revived and placed in the middle of this northern city to mock us. There they were again – the twisted mouths, the angry eyes, the cries of 'nigger' and other racial epithets, the derisive watermelons held aloft by young men wearing Ku Klux Klan tee-shirts." Ira Glasser of the ACLU wrote about how the "good people" of Bensonhurst stayed at home during the marches, thereby missing out on "an opportunity for redemption, a chance to reject, by their witness, the culture of racism – which inevitably begets environments hospitable to lynchings."

Later, Judge Owens sentenced Fama and Mondello to maximum prison terms for their roles in the murder of Yusuf Hawkins. Fama received a sentence of 32 years-and-eight months to life, while Mondello was sentenced to a term of five years-four months to 16 years.

The trial of Joseph Vento followed. His lawyer announced that Vento had reneged on his promise to testify for the prosecution because he had been threatened by the family of Joseph Fama, whom he suggested had organized crime connections. At the trial, four Blacks from Dayton, Ohio, where Vento once lived, were brought in to testify that he was free of racial prejudice. A jury acquitted Vento of intentional murder but could not reach a verdict on a second murder charge and a charge of riot. Therefore, he was scheduled to be tried again, this time along with Joseph Serrano. Vento was later sentenced to a term of two years-eight months to eight years for unlawful imprisonment.

Charles Stressler, who was charged with second-degree murder and several misdemeanors, was tried next, along with Steven Curreri, who was charged with assault, riot, and criminal possession of a weapon. Again, they were tried in the same courtroom by separate juries. At this trial, Stressler admitted that he had delivered a box of baseball bats to the mob that had gathered the night of the murder, but he said they were for defensive purposes. A mistrial was declared in his case when juror Lydia Bermudez screamed at Moses Stewart, Hawkins' father, for "staring at me." She said she felt threatened and could no longer be a fair juror in the case. Both Curreri and Stressler were ultimately acquitted of all charges.

The fifth and sixth trials in the Bensonhurst case involved John Vento, James Patino, and Joseph Serrano. There were two juries in the courtroom, one for Vento, one for Patino and Serrano. The judge dismissed the most serious charge (murder) against Serrano and said the prosecution's evidence against both defendants was so weak that any murder or manslaughter convictions would be thrown out. After deliberating for less than four hours, the jurors in the Patino and Serrano case acquitted the defendants of all major charges. Patino was acquitted of all charges, but Serrano was convicted of weapons possession. He was sentenced to 300 hours of community service, fined $1,000, and sentenced to three years probation for the weapons possession charge. Vento was acquitted of the second-degree murder charge but was convicted of riot. For this conviction, he was sentenced to one-and-one-third to four years, which, since it was to be served concurrently with his previous sentence for unlawful imprisonment, added no additional time.

After the jury verdicts in the Vento and Serrano trials, Reverend Al Sharpton and others planned a march in Bensonhurst to protest the light sentences. The march was cancelled when Sharpton was stabbed in the chest as the marchers assembled. Bensonhurst resident Michael Riccardi, 27, was arrested and charged with attempted murder, criminal possession of a weapon, and civil rights violation. The march resumed the following day. There was no violence, but typically, the residents of the community expressed the sentiment that the minister got what he deserved.

The last of the Bensonhurst trials, that of Pasquale Raucci, who was charged with second-degree murder, manslaughter, assault, and several misdemeanors, ended some 20 months after the murder of Yusuf Hawkins. Raucci was acquitted of murder and manslaughter but convicted of riot, illegal imprisonment, weapons possession, and menacing. The judge set aside the guilty verdict on the riot charge because of insufficient evidence. Thus ended the Bensonhurst trials.

THE AFTERMATH

But the debate continued, leaving many questions unanswered. The police estimated that a pack of at least 30 white Bensonhurst residents gathered on the evening of August 23, 1989, armed with baseball bats, handguns, and other weapons.

They attacked a 16-year-old Black youth and his three companions who were in the neighborhood in response to an advertisement for a used automobile. During the attack, Yusuf Hawkins was shot and killed. Of those in the mob, only eight were tried and one convicted of murder. Four others were convicted of lesser charges, and three were acquitted of all charges. The many trials failed to resolve the questions of who was to blame and exactly what happened. Many observers doubt that justice was served.

The evidence clearly showed that a mob of armed toughs gathered on 69th Street with the clear intent of doing harm to Blacks and Hispanics. Their language made their intentions clear. In addition, the evidence indicated that many (dozens and perhaps hundreds) residents of Bensonhurst witnessed the murder that night but refused to testify or conveniently forgot what they had seen. This wall of silence, together with community pressure and threats of retaliation, weakened the prosecution's case.

For the family and supporters of Yusuf Hawkins, the unfortunate outcome resulted in large measure from the ineffective performance of the prosecutors. Much of the case for the prosecution depended on the testimony of John Vento. He was supposed to have been the main witness for the prosecution, like Robert Riley had been in the Howard Beach case, but he was threatened with retaliation by organized crime. His testimony might have won the case for the prosecution.

In addition to the difficulty of proving which one of the 30 youths actually pulled the trigger, there were many other shortcomings in the prosecution's case. Gina Feliciano, another important witness, had a history of drug use, which damaged her credibility. Between the time of the shooting and the trial, she was again hospitalized for drug treatment. Two of the prosecution's witnesses were incarcerated for a variety of crimes and were not considered to be credible. Another had a long history of mental problems. Russell Gibbons, a Black man, testified that he had assisted in transporting the baseball bats used by the mob.

Regardless of the outcome of the trials, the supporters of Yusuf Hawkins, who protested by marching in the streets of Bensonhurst, exposed the racism so endemic to that community. Residents of the community demonstrated, for the world to see, through their distorted faces, vile language, and primitive symbolism, that racism in Bensonhurst is pervasive and capable of bringing forth extreme acts of violence. It further proved that even in the 1990s, there are still some communities in the United States in which young Black men must venture at their own risk.

The 1989 murder of 16-year-old Yusuf Hawkins in Bensonhurst was not unlike the 1955 lynching of 14-year-old Emmett Till in Mississippi. Emmett Till was ambushed and lynched by a pack of white men because he had whistled at a white woman. More than three decades later, Yusuf Hawkins was lynched in New York City by a mob of white men who thought erroneously that he was one of the Black men invited to a party by a local resident. In both cases, there was the explosive mixture of sex and race. For Emmett Till and Yusuf Hawkins, their skin color cost them their lives.

10

THE VIOLENCE CONTINUES

Following the racist mob attacks in Howard Beach in December 1986, New York City became a hotbed of racial violence. Some of the acts could be attributed to the so-called copycat phenomenon, wherein individuals reenact highly publicized events. Others, no doubt, reflected an intensified effort to reverse the minimal civil rights gains of minorities. No matter what the cause, the 1980s and 1990s have been difficult for New York's Black and Hispanic citizens. Racial violence has generated feelings of despair and hopelessness; the very existence of people of color has become increasingly a matter of chance. How can Blacks ride the New York subways without thinking that they will be mowed down like the four young men who were shot, without provocation, by Bernhard Goetz? Should Blacks venture into one of New York's ethnic enclaves, there is no way of knowing whether they will be murdered by a racist mob, as happened in Howard Beach and Bensonhurst. Nor can a Black male be sure that while walking down a street he will not be killed by some crazed racist person, as happened to so many Black men at the hands of Joseph Christopher.

Black males have considerably more to fear than females, for they have been the primary targets of racial violence, but as the deaths of Eleanor Bumpers, Yvonne Smallwood, and Mary Mitchell demonstrate, being Black and female can also be risky.

And then there is police brutality. It is one thing to be attacked by whites in the general population; it is quite another to meet racial violence at the hands of police officers. Yet, this has been the case much too often in New York City. The 1980s demonstrated that Blacks who fear random violence are far from paranoid, for they can never be sure from whom the next attack will come. For example, it is now common knowledge that back in 1983 and 1984, Black male passengers on New York's subways were being systematically arrested, falsely and improperly, by transit police officers who charged them with sexual attacks on white women. Not many persons were convicted, but several accepted plea-bargaining deals even though they were innocent. Indeed, the so-called victims did not even know they had been molested until they were summoned to appear in court.

The Howard Beach attack was one of the more gruesome in the history of the city. If such an event had happened in a truly civilized society, citizens would have become alarmed, and they would have expressed sympathy for the victim's family. But in the months following the attack, gangs of whites randomly attacked Blacks in rapid succession, clearly demonstrating their hatred and showing no remorse. While the victims were overwhelmingly male and the attackers were mainly citizens at large, Black females were also attacked, and white police officers were frequently the attackers, especially in cases of racial homicides. The murder of Eleanor Bumpers, the 66-year-old ailing grandmother, showed just how little regard for Black life the police have. And when police are repeatedly vindicated of any wrongdoing, as in the Michael Stewart case, a clear message is transmitted that it is O.K. to beat and kill Black people.

Incidents of racial violence following the Howard Beach attack were so widespread that a brief listing will be provided in chronological order, giving greatest attention to those resulting in the deaths of the victims.

. . .

Police officials reported that incidents of racial violence jumped more than 150 percent in the first month following the Howard Beach incident. The Bias Incident Investigating Unit of the police department reported that such attacks occurred at the rate of 10 per week, up from an average of 4 a week for the year before Howard Beach. Although these reports probably represent an under-numeration of such incidents, they do indicate that they increased in number.

In the early morning hours (circa 4:00am) of February 12,

1987, the police reported that they responded to a call about a burglary in progress in Forest Hills, Queens. A violent struggle ensued between Wajid Abdul-Salaam, a 35-year-old subway track worker, and eight police officers. The officers eventually restrained Abdul-Salaam with leg shackles and handcuffs and bound his hands and feet with medical tape. Six of the officers reportedly suffered minor injuries, but it was never explained why so many officers were needed to restrain one unarmed man.

Abdul-Salaam was then placed in a holding cell at the 112th precinct station in Forest Hills, where he lost consciousness. He was then taken to St. John's-Queens Hospital, where doctors pronounced him dead. The attorney for his family, C. Vernon Mason, charged that Abdul-Salaam was killed by the police. Mason further charged that preliminary findings of an autopsy performed by the Medical Examiner's office covered up the brutality of the police officers. The autopsy indicated that there was a high level of cocaine in Abdul-Salaam's body but "no significant physical injuries."

Although the Medical Examiner's office reported that it would stand by its original findings, Mason said he knew of a test at the hospital that demonstrated an absence of cocaine in Abdul-Salaam's body. He said Abdul-Salaam had been "brutalized, hog-tied and beaten to death." The Queens District Attorney's office maintained, however, that it found no evidence to suggest that police officers had acted improperly, and a hospital spokesperson claimed that no toxicology test was performed on Abdul-Salaam because an insufficient quantity of blood had been sent to the laboratory to perform such a test.

The final autopsy report of the Medical Examiner's office concluded that Abdul-Salaam died of "acute cocaine intoxication and occlusive coronary arteriosclerosis." The call by Reverend Herbert Daughtry for a special prosecutor and an independent autopsy went unheeded.

In the meantime, in late February 1987, a group of some ten white youths attacked and chased a group of 10 Black teenagers in Bayside, Queens. The Blacks were awaiting a public bus when they were attacked by the whites. Racial slurs were exchanged between them. A few days later, Thomas Pistorino telephoned a local newspaper and identified himself as one of the attackers. He was charged with attempted assault, reckless endangerment, and other crimes. Pistorino reportedly said that he had encouraged a group of friends to attack residents of Children's Village, a center for children with family or emotional problems. He said he sought revenge for beatings he had suffered at the hands of Blacks while a resident in one of the foster care homes.

Far more serious was the police killing of 27-year-old Nicholas A. Bartlett, a self-employed young man who had attended St. John's University, served in the Army, and had a wife and two small children. The shooting occurred on February 28, 1987, at about 10:00pm on 125th Street, a busy Harlem street. According to police officers, Bartlett attacked a policeman without warning or provocation, and when other officers appeared, he menacingly raised a 15-inch lead pipe

above his head. Suddenly and without provocation, he allegedly hit an officer 10 to 15 times with the pipe. An officer
radioed for assistance and then rescued the officer who was
attacked. Bartlett, it is said, attempted to strike the other
officers. The police officers then opened fire. Six of the 10
shots fired struck Bartlett in the head and body. He died two
hours later in Harlem Hospital. Three of the eight officers
involved were said to have been injured, none of them seriously.

Members of Bartlett's family, which included his wife, a
6-year-old son, and a 5-month-old daughter, challenged the
police version of the shooting. The police maintained that the
shooting had been justified because they believed that deadly
force was about to be used against them. They did not explain
how a man with a pipe could constitute a deadly threat to eight
officers with guns. Several witnesses, agreeing with the
family, claimed that Bartlett was not holding a pipe, nor was he
menacing the officers.

Shortly after the shooting, it was reported by the police
that Bartlett had gone to the police station twice the day he was
killed to complain of police harassment as he sold books,
incense, cassette tapes, jewelry, musk oil, and other items.
When he arrived at the police station to make his complaint, he
asked to see the commanding officer, who was out on patrol.
He then requested to see the community relations officer, who
was not on duty.

The shooting of Bartlett by police was called a "summary
execution" by Manhattan Borough President David Dinkins,

the highest-ranking Black elected official in city government. He said, "Our laws do not permit police officers to make a determination and then summarily execute on the spot." He added that the killing "raise[d] questions once again in the minds of the public about the conduct of the entire New York Police Department in minority neighborhoods." "You can't tell me that eight police officers, trained police officers with weapons, with clubs, have an inability to disarm one man with a pipe without shooting," Dinkins concluded.

Two months after the killing, a grand jury found that the police officers had committed no crime on February 28. According to the Manhattan District Attorney, the grand jury met 21 times and heard testimony from 49 witnesses. The police commissioner maintained that the officers had acted within departmental guidelines.

Nicholas Bartlett, who was born in Jamaica, came to New York at the age of six. Some members of his family in New York were Black nationalists, and his grandfather had a large library of books on Black nationalism and African history. As a child he read widely and was taught to speak Swahili by his grandmother. He had no arrest record, and according to people who knew him, he was a nonviolent person, even-tempered and retiring. His killing occurred two days after the acquittal of the police officer who shot and killed Eleanor Bumpers and less than one month after the death of Wajid Abdul-Salaam.

According to other vendors in the area, the police had increased their surveillance and harassment of street vendors in

Harlem that day. As one vendor put it, "I wasn't even allowed to set up even though I have a license. Police were intimidating that day, bullying people up and down the avenue, shaking people up. It seemed unusual and it was an intense campaign against Black people who were trying to sell that day." Meanwhile, several witnesses who had not testified before the grand jury came forward. They maintained that the police did not give Bartlett a chance to surrender before killing him.

In an incident that was not considered racial by the police, on the night of April 20, 1987, a house in Flushing, Queens, was burned. The house had been rented by the city as a home for six border babies—infants who had been abused, neglected, or abandoned in hospitals. These babies are virtually all Black or Hispanic, and the incident, described by the police as arson, was an attempt to keep the babies out of the neighborhood. The police maintained that one of the defendants entered the house to set the fire with a flammable liquid. Those charged in the case were 41-year-old Rita Amato, her 45-year-old husband Philip Amato, 55-year-old Michael Scotto, 62-year-old Ugo Serrone, and 41-year-old James Raffa. They all lived on the same block as the children's home. Although the case was not officially entered as one based on racial bias, the actions of the neighborhood residents were seen by Blacks and Hispanics as racist. Despite the defendants' statements to the contrary, one of their lawyers, Jacob Eversoff, insisted that his clients were being persecuted because the Mayor wanted to "ingratiate himself with certain groups." When asked by a reporter which groups he had in mind, he responded "minority groups."

According to the prosecutor in the case, two of the witnesses for the prosecution received anonymous threatening letters and verbal harassment from two of the five defendants. One such message, a post card, said, "You are a Riley like in Howard Beach. You stink. And you will get yours." The five defendants were convicted of third-degree arson, three by a jury and two by a judge. Their conviction was largely based on the testimony of Joseph Minchella, who agreed to wear a listening device in conversations with the suspects.

The summer of 1987 began with the police killing another Black man. On June 20, Terrence Keane, a 20-year-old mechanic, was shot by officers on routine patrol in North Bronx. According to police, the victim was driving in the opposite direction from a police vehicle when his car plowed into the left side of the police vehicle. Both cars shifted into reverse gear, at which time the victim's car slammed into the back of the police car and the bumpers locked. Keane's car then rammed a parked car before coming to a stop. One officer got out of the police vehicle with his gun drawn; the other officer attempted to remove Keane from the passenger side of his car. When both officers attempted to remove him, a struggle ensued, causing the gun of one of the police officers to discharge.

Keane was taken to Our Lady of Mercy Hospital, where he died. An autopsy found that he died of a gunshot wound to the abdomen. Officials of the Medical Examiner's office reported that the victim had a small vial of crack lodged in his larynx. Word of Keane's death brought protesters to the scene

231

of the incident, charging the police with the excessive use of force.

The rest of the summer remained relatively free of extreme racial violence. However, on September 2, three Black youths on their way home from their jobs as stock clerks at a supermarket were attacked by a group of 20 white youths wielding baseball bats, a pipe, and a fluorescent bulb. Additionally, the white youths shouted racial slurs. The attack took place in the predominantly white section of Canarsie, Brooklyn at about 11:00pm.

The Black youths had walked to a bus stop and were waiting for two female co-workers. A white youth emerged from a small park and called out to the Blacks. Thinking that the person who called was a co-worker, they started to cross the street. Suddenly, the mob of white youths shot out from the park with baseball bats and sticks and chased the Blacks. When they caught up with them, they beat them. One of the youths rode his bicycle to a gypsy cab stand a block away and telephoned the police.

The Black youths were 17-year-old Evan Lawrence, 19-year-old David Smiley, and 19-year-old Michael Washington. The three were treated at a hospital for cuts and bruises and then released. One required four stitches for a cut on his head. One suspect, 17-year-old Alphonso Petti, a plumber's helper, was arrested and charged with second-degree assault, first-degree incitement to riot, harassment, and violation of the state's civil rights law.

The following week, on September 9, three Black teenagers and two Hispanic youths were chased out of a Brooklyn park in Carroll Gardens by a group of 10 white youths, who attacked them with a stick and a bottle. The minority youths had come to the park to play basketball. The whites told them they should leave, but when they started to go, they were chased and beaten by the whites. One of the victims, who was struck in the head with a stick, was given five stitches at a hospital and released.

The following day, September 10, a Black teenager, Robert Williams, and another youth were distributing Sears, Roebuck and Company advertising fliers to homes in a largely white section of Ozone Park. They were accosted by a group of five or six white teenagers. An argument ensued, and Williams was struck on the head with a baseball bat. He suffered skull fractures.

Yvonne Smallwood, a 28-year-old Bronx working mother of four children, died on December 9 at a hospital in Elmhurst, Queens after having been arrested by police on December 3. Three white police officers, two of them women, arrested her when she protested a summons issued to her companion, 43-year-old Austin Harper, that he alledgedly lacked proper insurance. The police claimed that she bit and kicked the officers, injuring all of them. Her companion and lawyers for the family charged that she was severely beaten by the police.

After her arrest, Yvonne Smallwood spent the last six days of her life shuttling between Rikers Island prison, the courts, and city hospitals. She spent some hours at North

Central Bronx Hospital, but was returned to police custody in the early morning hours of December 4. In the next five days, she went from booking at criminal court in the Bronx to detention at Rikers Island to treatment at the infirmary there. Then she was sent to the hospital, where she was released and sent to a court hearing. She was returned to Rikers Island, referred again to the infirmary there for weakness and dizziness, and finally sent back to the hospital, where she died at 5:10pm on December 9.

According to the autopsy report, Yvonne Smallwood died from a massive blood clot in her leg. However, members of her family maintain that she died of injuries caused by the police, who repeatedly hit and kicked her on at least two different occasions. Reports were contradictory: some witnesses claimed she was beaten by the police; others said she had attacked the police. Smallwood's sister, a nurse who visited her in the hospital, said she was told that the injuries resulted from a police beating.

At Yvonne Smallwood's funeral, the minister who delivered the eulogy asked, "Why are we here?" The answer: "Because the New York City Police Department has participated in another execution of one of our loved ones."

On Christmas day, two Black men were beaten by a group of whites in the Bensonhurst section of Brooklyn. According to police, shortly before 11:00pm, Steven LaMont, 31, and Sylvester LaMont, 29, were collecting redeemable bottles and cans. They passed a group of 7 to 10 whites standing by a double-parked car. The whites said, "What's in the cart, niggers, are you robbing houses?" The brothers were chased, and when they were caught, the whites beat them with sticks. An anonymous call to the police emergency number brought officers to the scene.

At a press conference, the two brothers described what happened: "They were coming from all angles like a wolf pack, rearing over cars, dodging in between cars, coming from behind vans, in front of vans," said Steven LaMont. They said that the group of whites attacked them with sticks, a marble slab, and a knife. They were saved from serious injury by three young white women who were with other persons who witnessed the attack.

The two brothers were treated at a local hospital. Douglass Malliband, 19, was arrested and charged with second-degree assault, possession of a dangerous instrument, and violating the federal civil rights act. A second suspect, 17-year-old Dean Presita, was arrested later and charged with the same offenses.

Finally, on December 29, 39-year-old Alfred Sanders was killed by two white police officers in Laurelton, Queens. According to police, Sanders, whom they described as emotionally disturbed, lunged at them with a knife. The two policemen fired a total of 11 shots at Sanders, who died at Mary Immaculate Hospital of multiple gunshot wounds to the stomach region.

The police officers had responded to a telephone call from Sanders' companion, Elease Watson, who reported that he was threatening her. Before the officers arrived, Sanders reportedly broke a window in the front door and uprooted the mailbox. He was calling for his son, who was with his mother, Elease Watson. He threatened to commit suicide.

Although the police said witnesses confirmed the official account of the shooting, a woman who witnessed the incident said, "He had his hands in the air and he took four steps toward the police, and they opened fire." She reported that Sanders had been unarmed. A grand jury found no basis for criminal charges against the two police officers. A spokesman for the NAACP termed the panel's finding "outrageous" and asked the Governor to appoint a special prosecutor to investigate the case. The NAACP spokesman insisted that Sanders did not either threaten or lunge at the officers at any point during the altercation.

According to police department regulations, the shooting of Alfred Sanders should not have happened. The department had introduced additional weapons – including a five-foot plastic shield and a special water cannon that can immobilize people – to subdue agitated people while protecting police officers at the same time. The police officers involved in the Sanders case telephoned the precinct for the protective devices, but the officer in charge was on another call. A second unit equipped with the devices, the Emergency Service Team, was also called, but it arrived minutes after the shooting.

The year 1987 was one of racial violence, including police killings of at least four Black men and one Black woman. Many more were injured. In addition, one Black man, a 33-year-old student from Ethiopia, was found on March 12 hanging mysteriously from a tree in Central Park with his hands and legs loosely bound. The police reported that they did not think this was a racial murder, and the cause of death was listed as an apparent suicide. However, the question must be asked, How could a man tie his own legs and hands and then hang himself?

On Sunday, 30 January 1988, shortly after the beginning of another year of racial violence, 40-year-old Juan Rodriguez met his death while in police custody in Brooklyn. According to police, Rodriguez, the father of three children, became violent and threatened neighbors. He died in an ambulance after having been restrained by four police officers and four emergency service officers. One of the police officers claimed they had restrained Rodriguez with handcuffs to prevent further flailing.

The police had responded to an emergency call from a neighbor of the victim, who charged that Rodriguez was threatening neighbors and banging on doors. When the emergency medical service officers arrived, they strapped Rodriguez to a hospital stretcher before removing him from the apartment. The Medical Examiner's autopsy report showed that Rodriguez's death was caused in part by blunt-force injuries. In addition, two other causes of death were reported: "acute agitation" and "occlusive coronary arteriosclerosis." The Latino Coalition for Racial Justice maintained that Rodriguez was murdered when four police officers brutally beat him.

In early March, three white men were arrested in the Bronx for attacking Black people. They were charged with beating a Black woman who had refused to have sex with them and of then randomly striking other Blacks in the area. Altogether, five people were injured in the attacks, which took place on March 3 at about 3:00am. The Black woman was reportedly a prostitute who was offered $10 for sexual acts. When she refused, one man jumped from the car and hit her with a baseball bat, shouting, "That's what niggers get."

According to police, the men then went on a rampage, injuring four other people in the West Farms section of the Bronx. After beating the woman, they attacked about a dozen people awaiting a bus, striking them with a baseball bat and a tree limb. They also robbed one person. The arrested men were 18-year-old Steven Carr, 20-year-old Lawrence Marias, and 18-year-old Shawn Murray. They were arrested when a victim gave the police the license plate number of their car. Inside the car, the police found the bat and the tree limb. The suspects were charged with assault, robbery, aggravated harassment, violation of civil rights, and criminal possession of weapons. Two of their victims were taken to a local hospital, along with the woman, 27-year-old Euvelia Poindexter, who suffered two broken arms and a dislocated wrist. Another, 19-year-old Israel Velazguez, suffered a fractured left hand and lacerations of the skull.

In May, two white police officers were charged with the beating of a homeless Black man outside Madison Square Garden on February 20. The officers were off-duty when the attack occurred and were returning from a basketball game. According to prosecutors in the case, after the basketball game, the officers went to a nearby bar. Outside the bar, they encountered 33-year-old Touissant Vogelsung. An argument escalated to the point where the officers punched and kicked the victim. A homeless bystander, Rodney Grant, intervened on Vogelsung's behalf, hitting one of the officers on the head with a two-by-four. When Grant fled, the officers chased Vogelsung, and upon reaching Vogelsung, they struck him on the head and beat him with a bottle. At no time did the officers identify themselves as policemen. Vogelsung spent 11 days in a hospital, where he was treated for a broken jaw, two broken ribs, and a collapsed lung.

On May 22, two minority youths were beaten by a group of whites outside their apartment house in the Bronx. According to police, 20-year-old Ryan Henriques was hit on the head with a metal pipe. His cousin, 17-year-old Darren Henry, was punched in the mouth. They ran into the apartment house and locked the door, but one of the attackers poked a hole through the glass and opened it. A suspect, Massimo Caruso, was arrested and charged with first-degree assault.

Derek Antonio Tyrus was 17 years old when he died after being hit by a car on October 17, 1988, in Staten Island. The police said he might have been chased to his death by a group of white males with whom he had engaged in an argument. The incident was reminiscent of the Howard Beach killing two years earlier.

This encounter took place in a section of Staten Island known as Rosebank, a predominantly Italian American working-class community. A group of 10 Black teenagers, ranging from 11 to 18 years old, encountered a white man who was standing near the entrance to a bar. The police reported that one of the teenagers noticed the man staring at them and asked, "What are you looking at? What are you doing in this neighborhood? You don't belong here.

At least one other man emerged from the bar, and the argument continued as the teenagers ran and scattered. They were pursued by two cars, one of them driven by one of the men with whom they had argued. At one point, an occupant of one of the cars got out and pushed one of the youths to the sidewalk. According to the police, "The last time Antonio Tyrus was observed, he was just north of the bar. We don't really have a good handle on what happened to them."

However, Tyrus was hit by a car driven by Stanford Levy, who stopped as soon as he realized that he had hit someone. Levy was not part of the group with whom the teenagers had engaged in the argument. Tyrus, who was a senior at New Dorp High School, was taken to St. Vincent's Hospital, where he died about one hour later.

Rosebank is a community similar to Bensonhurst and Howard Beach. But unlike those communities, many of the residents of Rosebank are Black and live in public housing projects. According to an official of the Staten Island chapter of the NAACP, only one racially-motivated crime (a house was burned) had received a felony conviction since he first moved there in 1948 — although there had been dozens of reports of such incidents and several arrests. Racist graffiti, such as "Death to All Niggers" and "KKK," can be seen throughout the Rosebank neighborhood.

The Staten Island District Attorney ruled on November 23 that the death of Derek Antonio Tyrus was not racially motivated and that no charges would be filed in the case. He stated that the case would not be presented to a grand jury because there was no evidence to support allegations of bias or criminality.

Richard Luke, a 25-year-old unemployed handyman who shared an apartment with his mother and sister in a public housing project in the Long Island City section of Queens, died after being arrested by housing police officers. The confrontation took place on May 22, 1989, when Luke ran into the apartment complaining that he was having difficulty breathing. His mother, Patricia Garcia, asked if he wanted to go to a hospital, but he said that he did not and ran out of the apartment. His sister called for an ambulance.

A housing police unit was dispatched to assist the paramedics. Garcia claimed that she saw her son run in the building and then come out. "The next thing I know, I hear this big commotion downstairs," she said. She then ran downstairs to find the two housing police officers struggling with her son on the floor. She said, "They had him down. I screamed, 'Don't hit him. He's sick. He needs help.'"

Meanwhile, the officers called for back-up support, and some six additional police arrived. They took Luke to the lockup section of the station house. His mother said she followed and found her son screaming. "They said he had gone crazy, and was banging his head on the floor. They were laughing," she recalled. An ambulance arrived to take Luke to the hospital. When Garcia arrived there she said, "The doctor came out and told me, 'your son is dead.' "

Angry residents of the housing project protested the death of Richard Luke, charging police with excessive use of force. Some 200 residents marched to the housing police station and then to the Queensboro Bridge, delaying traffic on both sides. Other protests that followed were joined by people from throughout the city. These protests took place because Luke was well liked in the community.

The Medical Examiner's office reported that Luke had died of "acute cocaine intoxication," but family members and neighbors insisted that he did not use cocaine. A lawyer for the family asked for an investigation of the death and filed a lawsuit charging wrongful death. Seven months later, a state investigation found that Richard Luke did not die from cocaine intoxication, but from "asphyxia by obstruction of the larynx by ascription of gastric contents while face-up in a restraint blanket used to control his violent behavior following cocaine use." That is, he choked on vomit while wrapped in the restraint blanket.

A mentally retarded man, 31-year-old Kevin Thorpe, died on July 10, 1989, in a struggle with police officers. Thorpe stopped breathing after at least four officers subdued him in the apartment he shared with his mother in Brooklyn. His mother, Esther Thorpe, called police asking for help because her son was beating her with his fists, the police said. The first two officers at the scene could not subdue Thorpe and called for reinforcements. He died when officers laid on him and cut off his breathing, according to the Medical Examiner's office.

The police reported that Thorpe had become agitated and, when asked to sit down, he responded by punching and kicking them. Under such circumstances, the Emergency Medical Unit is usually called to assist, but for some unknown reason, the officers called for police reinforcements. A sergeant and several additional officers appeared, and they helped handcuff Thorpe and tied his legs together. The police said the struggle ended with Thorpe being held face down on the floor by four officers.

The police then called for an ambulance, but by the time it arrived, Thorpe had ceased breathing. He died in the emergency room of Long Island College Hospital. The autopsy report declared that "Kevin Thorpe was asphyxiated as the result of chest compression" while being restrained by police officers. "Natural disease neither caused nor contributed to his death," the report concluded. In explaining the diagnosis, a representative of the Medical Examiner's office said, "They were lying on top of him, and they compressed his chest so much that he could not breathe."

The lawyer for the Thorpe family, Colin Moore, claimed that four witnesses told him that police officers beat Thorpe with night sticks after knocking him down. "They were sitting on his chest, jumping on different parts of his body," Moore said. "The [autopsy] report makes it clear that Kevin Thorpe died as a direct result of police violence." One witness, a 13-year-old niece of the victim, said the officers beat Thorpe for about 15 minutes while he was handcuffed, and when relatives pleaded with the police to stop, they were told to move away.

Kevin Thorpe was one of seven children. He attended a school for the mentally handicapped from the age of 16 until his death. Family members and neighbors described him as friendly and childlike, inarticulate and reclusive. He enjoyed playing with children. Apparently, he did not understand what the officers meant when they asked him to calm down. His sister said he could feed and clothe himself but was unable to find his way home if he went out alone. She said his vocabulary consisted of only a few phrases. He was described as nonviolent and had never hit anyone before he slapped his mother.

Police department guidelines require that unless a disturbed person poses a threat to himself or others, regular patrol officers are to isolate the person and summon a supervisor and the Emergency Medical Services Unit. This procedure, adopted after the death of Eleanor Bumpers, was not followed in this case. Still, the grand jury voted not to indict anyone in the killing of Kevin Thorpe.

Henry Hughes, 25, died in police custody in the Bronx on September 9, 1989. The incident began with a purse-snatching on the subway platform, and police officers arrived on the scene to investigate. Altogether, eight officers from both the transit police force and the city were involved. They heard an injured woman scream and identified a man fleeing the scene, Henry Hughes, as her assailant.

The officers arrested Hughes after linking his wrists behind him with two lengths of handcuffs; they held his neck and legs with their feet. They then asked another officer to fetch some strips to bind his legs, but by the time the strips arrived, Hughes was bleeding. He was pronounced dead shortly thereafter.

Witnesses to the incident charged the police with using excessive force, but it was later ruled that the force used was not excessive. One witness reported that Hughes was beaten in the groin, on the head, and on other parts of his body. When asked by bystanders to stop the beating, it was reported that one officer drew his gun on the bystanders. While being beaten, Henry Hughes, who was unarmed, was said to have cried, "Help me, help me." But the police continued to beat him, according to one witness, who said, "They were treating him like an animal."

In just seven days, New York City police officers shot and killed three teenagers, and in the first nine weeks of 1990, they killed a total of 11 people. The first teenager to be killed in 1990 was 17-year-old Louis Liranso, who had arrived two months earlier from the Dominican Republic. Louis Liranso had come to New York City because he wanted to complete high school and study engineering. Unable to find employment, he spent his time on the streets with friends. Although he was unarmed, Liranso was shot in the back in Brooklyn as a police officer attempted to arrest him on January 27.

LEST WE FORGET: WHITE HATE CRIMES

Two police officers, responding to a radio call that four men with guns were engaged in a dispute, arrived at the site and found Liranso and another man arguing and wrestling on the sidewalk next to a Chinese restaurant. Liranso reportedly had been drinking heavily and flirting with the other man's sister.

According to police, the two officers seized Liranso and turned him over to another officer. One of the officers, it was maintained, had the suspect at gunpoint by a wall when he lowered his hands and turned toward her. She then shot Liranso, who was pronounced dead at Woodhull Hospital. Several witnesses contested the police version, however. They maintained that the officer was walking with the suspect, who had his hands in the air, into the restaurant when the shot was fired.

Four days later, on January 31, a police officer shot and killed 14-year-old Jose Luis Lebron five blocks from where Louis Liranso was killed (in the Bushwick section of Brooklyn). According to police, Lebron had been accused of stealing $10 from a man. The robbery reportedly occurred at Maria Hernandez Park, renamed to honor a neighborhood resident who had been active in the fight against drugs. (She is said to have been killed by drug dealers.) The robbery victim flagged a police car and reported that he had been robbed of $10 by two teenagers. The police and the robbery victim cruised the neighborhood looking for the teenagers. When they spotted them, a police officer got out of the car and grabbed one of them, Edward Garcia. Lebron ran down the street and was chased by the police in the patrol car. As they closed in on him, he turned and ran toward them. when, he reached into his jacket and pulled at a zipper, the officer fired twice, hitting him in the head. He was pronounced dead at the scene. The officer said he thought Jose Luis Lebron had a gun. Later, Lebron was found to be unarmed.

Scores of neighborhood residents gathered outside the local police station to protest the killings of the unarmed teenagers. They were later joined by people from other parts of the city. The officer who shot Lebron, Frank Albergo, was well known to teenagers in the community, who claimed he constantly harassed them. According to his mother, Jose Luis Lebron was a good student at a local intermediate school and wanted to become a lawyer.

On February 2, a police officer shot and killed 13-year-old Robert Cole in the East Harlem section of Manhattan. Cole, a suspect in a robbery, was carrying a gun at the time. According to the police, Cole and two other persons surrounded a 42-year-old truck driver inside a bodega. One of the suspects grabbed the victim from behind, around the neck, as Cole flashed a gun and tried to rob him. The victim resisted, wrestled the gun away from Cole, and chased the fleeing suspects into the street.

The victim found two police officers in a patrol car, who soon caught up with and cornered Cole. The officers ordered Cole to drop the gun, and when he refused, one of them shot him in the chest.

Cole was known in the community as a drug dealer, and doctors at Harlem Hospital said they found 35 vials of crack in his clothing after he died there. He had attended the Children's Storefront, an alternative school in the neighborhood, but officials there said he had stopped attending classes some two or three years earlier.

A police officer shot and killed a woman inside her apartment on November 3, 1990, after she approached him with his nightstick, which had fallen to the floor as they struggled. The police claimed that they had responded to one of three emergency calls to investigate what was described as a "violent fight" between 41-year-old Mary Mitchell and her 18-year-old daughter, Tiffany. When they arrived, they said Mitchell was going after her daughter, who was wielding a metal cane. When the officers tried to stop the fight, they reported that other family members pelted them with dishes and vases. Three officers detained these family members in one room while another officer, Arno Herwerth, subdued Mitchell in another. Roportedly, however, Mary Mitchell reportedly broke away and ran into another room. Herwerth tried to secure the door to that room with his nightstick, but somehow the door opened. When it did, the nightstick fell to the floor. Mitchell picked it up and started swinging at Herwerth, who then fired one shot at her. Mitchell was taken to Lincoln Hospital in the Bronx where she was pronounced dead.

According to the police, Mary Mitchell was swinging the nightstick "like a baseball bat. There's no question that he felt afraid for his life," Mitchell was 5'4" tall and weighed 170 pounds; Officer Herwerth was 6'0" tall and weighed 180 pounds.

The police arrested three members of the family on a variety of charges, including disorderly conduct, resisting arrest, and obstructing governmental administration. According to family members, the police overreacted to a domestic quarrel and tried to cover up their violence by charging family members.

Five New York City police officers were charged in the death of 21-year-old Federick Pereira, who died of injuries sustained while in police custody on February 5, 1991. They were charged with second-degree murder, manslaughter, assault, and criminally negligent homicide. The Medical Examiner's office ruled Pereira's death a homicide.

According to police, a struggle began just after officers approached the car in which Pereira slept. He was in the back seat of the car with the inside light on; a window was broken, and the license number of the car was listed as stolen. Two officers, James McMorrow and Thomas Loefell, were joined by three others, Barry Goldblatt, John O'Connel, and Anthony Paparella. They surrounded the car and knocked on the window. One of them put his hand through the broken window to unlock the door.

The police maintained that Pereira became violent as they removed him from the car. Once outside, he was handcuffed, after which he was forced to the ground and banged his head on the asphalt. They maintained that they did not use night sticks on Pereira and that there were no witnesses to the encounter.

When the Emergency Medical Service ambulance arrived, Pereira had facial injuries and his heart was not beating. He was pronounced dead at St. John's Hospital shortly thereafter. The police say they found a used crack pipe and a small amount of marijuana in his clothes. Records indicate that he had been arrested for selling drugs, larceny and unauthorized use of vehicles.

The five police officers, who were arrested on March 20, pleaded not guilty to the charges levied against them in connection with Pereira's death. An initial inquiry shortly after the death found that the officers had acted within police guidelines. This report relied solely on the officers' accounts of what happened. However, three witnesses came forward and cast doubt on the account of the officers. They testified that Pereira had been struck and that at some point one officer placed his hands around the victim's throat. Because of their testimony and the Medical Examiner's ruling that Pereira was choked to death, the Queens District Attorney, John J. Santucci, charged the five officers with murder.

In announcing the charges against the officers, Santucci said that one officer had choked Pereira as he lay face-down with his hands cuffed behind his back. "They had no right to take his life," Santucci said. "The victim was not in the violent throes of cocaine reaction," as the police had maintained. On the other hand, the police officers insisted that Pereira "went into a frenzy trying to resist arrest. He was finally rear-cuffed and placed lying down on the sidewalk adjacent to the suspect's car. While Pereira was lying on the sidewalk, he continued to struggle and kick at the officers." They contended that during the struggle, one officer radioed for another officer, who arrived and put restraining straps on the victim's ankles. At that point, Pereira ceased to move and an ambulance was called, they noted.

Although only one officer reportedly choked Pereira, the District Attorney claimed that all of the officers acted in concert because the police "all had some physical contact with him." Consequently, all were charged with murder.

However, three witnesses – Ronald Harmon, Anthony Hickok, and Thomas Zaribisky – testified that one officer hit Pereira with a night stick as he lay on the ground and that another sat on Pereira's back and pulled him backward by the neck. These three youths had spent the evening cruising in their car when they noticed the police brutalizing Pereira. They said they watched from about 20 feet away as the police beat and kicked Pereira, who was handcuffed with one leg tied to the handcuffs behind his back.

When the officers were arraigned, a large crowd of off-duty police officers gathered on the courthouse grounds and chanted, "Santucci must go! No justice, no service." During the proceedings, they packed the courtroom.

Federico Pereira was born in New York City two months after his father died in an automobile crash while serving in the Army in Texas. His mother later married a well-known salsa singer, Tito Nieves, whom the young Pereira frequently accompanied on tours. As as adullt, Pereira lived with his parents, although he was the father of a young son. He and the mother of his son later moved to northern New Jersey. At the time of his death, he was working as a cook in a fast food restaurant. His mother recalled that Pereira wanted to join the National Guard during the war against Iraq in the Persian Gulf but was rejected because of his criminal record.

In an unusual set of circumstances, the District Attorney who brought the charges against the five police officers retired shortly afterward, and his successor withdrew the charges against the officers.

. . .

These cases represent only a few of the acts of anti-minority violence in New York City in the first months after the murder of Michael Griffith in Howard Beach. It is by no means an exhaustive list, and it concentrates on those cases that resulted in death. In the months following the Howard Beach case, anti-minority violence flared at an alarming pace. Such acts continue to be a part of the New York scene, and the likelihood is that they will persist.

Most of these fatalities resulted from actions taken by police from various agencies – the New York City Police Department, the Transit Authority police and the police employed by the Housing Authority. These people are employed to protect citizens, but far too often they murder the people they are paid to protect. Individuals who are sworn to uphold the law end up breaking it. Under these circumstances, citizens rightfully fear police.

THE VIOLENCE CONTINUES

Police offenders are rarely punished for the use of excessive force against citizens. Indeed, 14 New York City police officers faced charges in 10 incidents while on duty in the 1980s. One of the 14 was convicted, and 10 were acquitted. One trial ended in a hung jury, and two cases remain unresolved. These figures do not include citizens killed by housing and transit police.

11

THE END

For those who say that racism is declining in the United States, the preceding chapters demonstrate that the reverse is true. And while there is no complete list of victims of racial violence in New York City, we know that dozens of Black people were killed in racist attacks there, and hundreds more were injured, some of them permanently, during the 1980s. The attacks continue at an alarming pace.

Racially motivated attacks in New York City were more likely to be directed against Blacks than other minorities. Blacks were responsible for few such attacks. (Blacks who commit murder usually victimize other Black people.) Several Hispanics were victims of these attacks, but they tended to be dark-skinned people, as the deaths of Luis Rodriguez and Juan Rodriguez illustrate.

The "culture of racism," in which racial prejudice is taught to young children at home, in school, and on the streets, provides a hospitable environment for acts of racial violence. This was clearly demonstrated in both Howard Beach and Bensonhurst. The insular nature of these communities and the resistance of their inhabitants to social change contributed to the culture of violence.

When the demographic characteristics are examined, a picture of civilian and police violence against people of color begins to emerge. Police officers were much more likely to kill and maim Blacks and Hispanics than were ordinary citizens. Police officers are armed – and their weapons of destruction are readily available. In New York City, police officers are taught to "shoot for the largest center of mass" available to them. In an interview, former Police Commissioner Benjamin Ward stated, "Every Professional knows you shouldn't shoot unless you intend to kill somebody."[1] Police officers enter an occupation in which the use of force is institutionalized. They share the sentiments of the larger society about minorities. Their work brings them into constant contact with poorer citizens who inhabit neighborhoods where crime flourishes. Police work is in many ways frustrating. Thus, the poor and the powerless become easy targets for venting negative feelings. Furthermore, police are likely to come from communities within which the greatest racial prejudice is nurtured.

In acts of racial violence, the assailants were usually teenagers and young adults, the average age of civilian attackers being about 19. For example, the 12 persons charged in the Howard Beach attack ranged from age 16 to 19 at the time. The same was true of those who killed in Gravesend and Bensonhurst.

Males, more than females, were likely to engage in racial violence. In all the cases discussed, the attackers were males, although they were sometimes accompanied by females. In no case did the females participate in the attack, however. The same was true of lynchings in the South; females often encouraged the attackers but rarely, if ever, participated directly.

Civilian attackers usually had little formal education. The general pattern was that they were either highschool graduates or dropouts. The attacks in Howard Beach and Bensonhurst provided a few exceptions: some of those accused were college students at the time. It was unusual for college students to engage in racial attacks, although such violence increased significantly in the 1980s and the early 1990s. Prior to these decades, college students may have harbored racial prejudice, but they were not inclined to translate those attitudes into behavior.

Many who engaged in racial violence were from working-class backgrounds. This was true of the cases presented here, and it has been true historically. To use the example of Howard Beach, most of the assailants were from working-class families, and some of them had entered the work place themselves: one worked in a restaurant, another sharpened knives for a living, and another worked for a trucking company.

Racial violence historically has been the province of the working class, frequently as a result of competition for employment and housing. During the Draft Riots of 1863, striking workers attacked Blacks who were hired to replace them. When working-class whites shared the same neighborhoods with Blacks, racial violence was commonplace.

In neighborhoods populated by the working class, territoriality assumes great significance. The often-asked question, "What were they [the Blacks] doing in Howard Beach?" is customary. Parochial in outlook, they distrust outsiders, especially people of color. In some white working-class neighborhoods, it is unsafe for Black people to be on the streets at any time, but especially at night.

A high proportion of the white assailants discussed in this book were from families that practiced Roman Catholicism. This is what the Black Roman Catholic priest Lawrence Lucas said in December 1987 that annoyed so many city officials: "Those who are killing us in our homes, falsely arresting us in the subway, murdering us in the streets, come primarily from the Catholic persuasion."[2] His remarks, regardless of their accuracy, caused city officials and some religious leaders to denounce him as a racist. The spiritual leader of the Roman Catholic Archdiocese, John Cardinal O'Connor, rebuffed Lucas.

On Sunday, December 28, 1986, one week after the racial attack, Mayor Koch went to Our Lady of Grace Roman Catholic Church in Howard Beach in search of what he called an "honest and forthright" discussion about race relations.[3]

While there, he met extreme hostility from the worshippers. Some of them refused to enter the church when they learned that he was there, and others walked out as he stood in front of the congregation. The residents did not fail to let the Mayor, who is Jewish, know that he was not welcome in their church. "Let him go to a synagogue," one worshipper said. Voicing a familiar rationalization, one person asked, "Where are you when we women are going to work and we're being robbed and mugged, mainly from these poor underprivileged people coming into our neighborhood?" There were cheers from in the audience. Some of them wanted to know what the Blacks were doing in *their* neighborhood.

It is a rather widely held notion that religious organizations and leaders have an important role to play in reducing racial tensions. After the first massive protest march in Bensonhurst, Bishop Francis J. Mugavero of the Roman Catholic Diocese of Brooklyn questioned the decision of the religious leaders to conduct the march. He claimed that the march not only inflamed racial tensions, but laid unfair blame on the Bensonhurst community for the violence. "We cannot lose sight that Bensonhurst is a sound community with deep and basic family values."[4]

The *New York Times* hosted a discussion on race relations a few days after the murder in Bensonhurst. Participating in the discussion was a Black minister, Reverend Herbert Daughtry, pastor of the House of the Lord Pentecostal Church in the Boerum Hill section of Brooklyn, and Reverend Charles S.

Fermeglia, an associate pastor at St. Dominic's Roman Catholic Church in Bensonhurst. Daughtry's church has a largely Black congregation, while Fermeglia's parish is composed mostly of Italian Americans.[5] From their discussion, it was clear that the Black minister and the white priest had contrasting views on many issues involving race relations, and that they even had difficulty understanding each other. For example, when asked to evaluate the response of the Bensonhurst community to the murder of Yusuf Hawkins, Fermeglia said that the residents of the community were "acting on the defensive," that they would like the issue to end because "they don't want to continue to be branded with the name of racists." Daughtry said he was concerned about "an attempt to just quiet this thing and get it over with."

When asked to discuss the expressions of racism by the residents during the protest marches following Yusuf Hawkins' killing, Daughtry said, "That's the obvious, most blatant manifestation of racism. But you have to wonder how pervasive it is at a subtle level." He explained that he was not condemning the whole community, but noted that Blacks had been attacked by whites in Bensonhurst on several occasions in recent years, and that finally, after one assault, protesters had marched in the community. He said, "So you say, well, if the decent people would have come forward after the Lamont experience, and begun to sort of do a self-inventory and to kind of put things in place and to kind of work at this . . . you're driven to raise the question: Would Yusuf still be alive?"

THE END

Fermeglia responded by saying, "That march that happened in Bensonhurst did not touch the people of my parish and my neighborhood because it's in a completely different section, you know, of the area." When Daughtry asked him whether he meant that if someone is attacked in one part of Bensonhurst that people a few blocks away "don't relate to that?" "That's right," replied Fermeglia. "That's why we haven't gotten much response from the other parishes around the area. And even many of the synagogues."

On the origin of negative perceptions about Blacks, Daughtry said that churches have been the greatest contributors to the view that Blacks are inferior to whites. On the other hand, Fermeglia said television and the movies have been the major contributors because of their portrayals of Blacks. According to Daughtry, "White Christiandom should bear the greatest brunt of the criticism for helping formulate the perceptions of African people . . . Just the projection of God as White, and Jesus as White, the prophets and all the good guys White . . . so that it really is saying that the ultimate ruler is White, looks like us." Fermeglia responded, "To say that the church has perpetuated a lie is to not understand the importance of tradition in the church . . . A person taken from Italy brings with him his church, brings it into this country. So he perceives his church as it has been depicted in art, through music, through worship." Finally, he said, "You perceive your church through your background and where you have come from."

LEST WE FORGET: WHITE HATE CRIMES

The most spirited disagreement between the clergymen occurred at the end of the discussion when they were asked about the distinction between criminality in general and crimes of racial violence. Said Fermeglia, "We have become comfortable with making a distinction between racial violence and violence in general. The result is the same – murder, death, killings." Daughtry said, "To confuse criminal behavior with racist behavior, there is a difference. I mean, the end result may be that you've got a dead body, but unless you understand the difference, you're going to keep getting dead bodies." He continued, "It is one thing for a person to be killed because of his religion or her religion, his pigmentation . . . It is another thing for a person to be killed because somebody wants some money. The reason that that person may have to do with a whole lot of sociological, economic, political factors." Daughtry concluded, "If we keep on trying to put criminality and racism in the same bag and keep on linking Central Park to, say, Bensonhurst or to Howard Beach, we'll never get out of the woods." Fermeglia then said, "What changed my attitudes concerning the separation between racist and violent attacks is precisely the one attack in Central Park. This attack was not done by lowlifes. It was done by kids who were educated."

Somewhat controversial but by no means unimportant is the question of ethnicity. In the early Black settlements in New York City, the Black residents met with violence from the Irish who came to the city in the 1840s and 1850s. Historian Gilbert Osofsky has reported that "small but regular clashes ordinarily involving Negroes and the Irish were recorded in the New York press then. The antagonism between these two peoples was undoubtedly one of the harshest intergroup hatreds in American history."[6]

During the Draft Riots of 1863, the Irish, police as well as civilians, attacked Blacks randomly. The police force was predominantly Irish, and most often cooperated with the white assailants. During that time, Blacks in New York City expressed antagonism toward the Irish and foreigners in general. A Black journalist wrote, "It is to be regretted that in this land of Bibles where the outcasts – the scum of European society – can come and enjoy the fullest social and political privileges, the Native Born American with wooly hair and dark complexion is made the victim."[7]

The anger expressed by this journalist was a function of the status Irish immigrants were accorded in the United States, relative to that of Black people. Indeed, one European traveler in New York in the 1860s reported that Irish immigrants considered Blacks to be "a soulless race." "I am satisfied that some of these people would shoot a Black man as they would a hog," he wrote.[8] The *New York Age*, a leading Black newspaper of the time, noted that "It is quite remarkable how easily foreigners catch on to the notion to treat Afro-Americans disdainfully and contemptuously."[9] Such attitudes by Blacks and the Irish only intensified the antipathy between them.

After the Draft Riots, there was little violence between Blacks and the Irish in New York City, but during the race riot of 1900, such incidents were commonplace. Poor Irish immigrants lived in the mud flats and shanty towns of Harlem at the turn of the century. With the acquiescence of police, they attacked the area's newly settled Blacks. Irish youth groups prospered in Harlem. For example, the Canary Island Gang (named for the section of Harlem in which they lived) guarded its territory like an army when Blacks first moved into the neighborhood. Their turf was west of Eighth Avenue, from 138th Street to 148th Street. One early Black resident reported that "The Irish boys on Eighth Avenue wouldn't let the other races come on Eighth Avenue at all."[10]

If Irish Americans were the chief initiators of racial violence in the second half of the 19th century, this role was taken over by Italian Americans in the 20th century. In the late 19th century, Italians were the new immigrant group to move to Harlem. The affluence of the period passed them by. They were a poor minority, disliked by other residents of the area because of their cultural characteristics. A reporter commented that, "Here can be found the refuse of Italy making a poor living on the refuse from Harlem's ashbarrels."[11]

During the first half of the 20th century, Italians in New York made gains in their living standards, but they were less successful than the Irish and the Jews, many of whom had preceded them. This lack of social mobility was manifested by the neighborhoods in which they lived. They were concentrated in working-class and poor sections, and they maintained strong loyalties to family, church, and neighborhood. After the

Howard Beach and Bensonhurst attacks, residents of these communities boasted that theirs were Italian neighborhoods where outsiders, especially people of color, were viewed with suspicion.

The civilian attacks previously discussed – the murder of Black men by Joseph Christopher, the murder of Willie Turks in Gravesend, the murder of Samuel Spencer III in Coney Island, and the mob attacks at Howard Beach and Bensonhurst – were all led by Americans of Italian descent. In the latter cases, virtually all of the assailants were Italian Americans.

It is instructive that in Howard Beach, one of the most admired and respected residents is the reputed head of the Gambino crime family, Joseph Gotti. While the residents attribute much of the conventional crime in the neighborhood to Blacks who live elsewhere, they appear to have respect for the organized crime figures who live in their midst. Organized crime is said to play an even greater role in Bensonhurst, and some of the young men in both areas aspire to membership in crime organizations.

Residents of such neighborhoods resent the advancements that have been made by Blacks, as few as there are, through government-enforced affirmative action programs, and they charge that Blacks are advancing too rapidly. They appear to be reasonably content with their own status and thus are unable to understand minority discontent. Interviews with residents of Howard Beach and Bensonhurst reveal an abundance of stereotypes and other indicators of prejudice. For example, Black people are routinely referred to as "eggplants" and "the colored," both of which indicate a degree of racial prejudice.

After the Howard Beach attack, many other racial incidents occurred in various parts of New York City, frequently in neighborhoods where Italian Americans predominate. The most serious of these took place in Bensonhurst, but others occurred in similar neighborhoods throughout the city. For example, Italian Americans were responsible for the beatings of three Black men in Carnarsie (Brooklyn), two Black brothers in Bensonhurst, 10 Black teenagers in Bayside (Queens), and the burning of the infant home in Flushing (Queens).

Shortly after the Bensonhurst incident, Alan Weisman, producer of the CBS news program *60 Minutes,* wrote about his childhood in the Flatbush section of Brooklyn and compared this community with Bensonhurst.[12] Weisman remembered the weekly ritual in which a group of older kids gathered outside the gates of St. Rose of Lima School "to beat up the Jews, the kikes – those kids with the glasses, the black vests, the sloppy sideburns and the stupid hats." His classmates at St. Rose were "mostly Italians and Irish, sons and daughters of the working class."

Weisman wrote that "In the Irish households, the presence of a handful of Blacks at St. Rose was greeted largely with a shrug . . . But in the Italian households (I grew up in one), the mood was decidedly more passionate. Those *muligans* – eggplants in southern Italian dialect. Why don't they stay with their own?" Among other things, they feared the decline of property values. Weisman wrote that his grandfather, a brick-layer, frequently ranted at the dinner table about how the world had failed him. He had "once entertained thoughts of the priesthood. But his wife had failed him by bearing only daughters, and one of his daughters – my mother – had failed him by marrying a Jew."

Regarding the young people of Bensonhurst who greeted the protest marchers with watermelons and racial epithets, Weisman wrote, "I have a pretty good idea of what they heard and did not hear in their homes, their schools, their churches. I've been to their holiday meals where the prayers are said and the long table is loaded with food, where Auriellio [his grand-father] waves his jug and points to the eggplants and curses the muligans – curses them for showing up in a world that was not supposed to change."

Writing about his career as a professional football player with the Cleveland Browns, Jim Brown had this to say about the Italian American community in Cleveland: "Cleveland also had a place called Little Italy. Cleveland was a city divided, East Side and West Side, black and white. Blacks who went to Little Italy were often attacked. I could have scored twenty touchdowns Sunday afternoon; if I walked through Little Italy that evening I'd have been jumped. I'd have no 32 on my back, all they'd see was black."[13]

Both Weisman and Brown wrote about the racism en-demic in such communities, and Weisman exhibited a special kind of honesty that is needed to transform this society into a safe haven, one in which humane social values are heeded and where racism and bigotry, when they occur, are not tolerated by citizens at large and the leaders they elect. Indeed it was the Reagan Administration in Washington that created an atmosphere in which intolerance thrived. This feat was achieved by the denigration of civil rights, opposition to affirmative action or what has been called "corrective justice," and the massive reductions in funding for special programs aimed at improving the plight of people of color, the poor, and women. What President Reagan managed to do for the country as a whole, Mayor Koch duplicated in New York City. They both left legacies unworthy of a contemporary civilized society. No doubt, that will plague us well into the 21st century.

It is difficult to predict whether racial violence will diminish in the near future, even with a change in administrations in Washington. If the social climate becomes more sympathetic to the rights of minorities and women, it is likely that such attacks will subside. It is unlikely, however, that Blacks and other people of color will be free to walk the streets in neighborhoods peopled largely by working-class whites, in New York City or elsewhere in the country. So long as American society remains one in which human exploitation is the norm, it is likely that Blacks will remain victims.

REFERENCE NOTES

Chapter 1: THE SETTING
1. The *New York Times*, April 1, 1987, p. B1.
2. Karl E. Taeuber, *Racial Residential Segregation, 28 Cities, 1970-1980*, Madison, Wisconsin: Center for Demography and Ecology, 1983, p. 44.
3. Jervis Anderson, *Guns in American Life*, New York: Random House, 1984.
4. Kenneth Clark, *Dark Ghetto*, New York: Harper and Row, 1965, p. 11.
5. Gilbert Osofsky, *Harlem: The Making of a Ghetto*, New York: Harper and Row, 1963, p. 36.
6. Michael Harrington, *The Other America*, New York: Macmillan, 1963, p. 62.
7. *Youth in the Ghetto*, New York: Harlem Youth Opportunities Unlimited, 1964, pp. 101-106.
8. *Ibid.*, p. 120.
9. John Hope Franklin, *From Slavery to Freedom*, New York: Alfred A. Knopf, 1947.
10. See Alphonso Pinkney, *The Myth of Black Progress*, New York and London: Cambridge University Press, 1984.
11. The *New York Times*, May 24, 1988, p. A16.

Chapter 2: RACIAL VIOLENCE REVISITED: A LOOK AT THE 1980s
1. See, for example, Donald T. Regan, *For the Record: From Wall Street to Washington*, New York: Harcourt Brace Javanovich, 1988.
2. See Tony Monterro, "Wilson's Apologies for Racism," *Political Affairs*, March 1988, pp. 19-26.
3. William Wilson, *The Declining Significance of Race*, Chicago: University of Chicago Press, 1978.
4. Terrel Bell, *The Thirteenth Man: A Reagan Cabinet Memoir*, New York: The Free Press, 1988.

5. The *New York Times*, September 13, 1987, sec. 4, p. 4.
6. *Ibid.*, September 23, 1987, p. B1.
7. See, for example, Alphonso Pinkney, *The American Way of Violence*, New York: Random House, 1972.
8. The *New York Times*, September 23, 1987, p. B1.
9. *Ibid.*
10. *Ibid.*, November 1, 1987, sec. D, p. 6.
11. *Ibid.*
12. *Ibid.*
13. *Report of the National Advisory Commission on Civil Disorders*, New York: Bantam Books, 1968, p. 17.
14. See, for example, George Berkley, *The Democratic Policeman*, Boston: Beacon Press, 1969.
15. The President's Commission on Law Enforcement and Administration of Justice, *The Challenge of Crime in a Free Society*, Washington, D.C.: Government Printing Office, 1967.
16. Leslie Cockburn, *Out of Control: The Story of the Reagan Adminstration's Secret War in Nicaragua, the Illegal Arms Pipeline, and the Contra Drug Connection*, Boston: Atlantic Monthly Press, 1987.

NOTE: Chapters 3-10 are based largely on articles from the following editions of the *New York Times*. When additional references are used, they are listed in detail.

Chapter 3: MICHAEL GRIFFITH: HOWARD BEACH
December 21-31, 1986; January 1-22, 1987; February 3, 5, 10-12, 22-23, 26-27, 1987; March 2, 7, 10, 12-14, 18, 25, 1987; April 5, 1987; May 22, 1987; June 18, 1987; September 6, 15, 17, 20-22, 1987; October 2, 6, 8, 9-10, 14, 20-21, 23-24, 26-27, 1987; November 1, 3, 6, 13-14, 17-23, 26, 1987; December 1, 6-7, 9-14, 20-24, 27, 1987; January 3, 23, 1988; February 6, 11-12, 1988; May 24-26,

1988; June 7, 9, 14, 18, 22-24, 1988; July 3, 8-9, 12, 15-16, 1988; September 20, 1988; November 27, 29, 1990.

Additional information in Chapter 8 from the following:

1. The *City Sun*, February 25-March 3, 1987, p. 5; August 11, 1987, p. 5.
2. *Frontline*, January 19, 1987, p. 1.
3. Joseph P. Fried, "Life's Nightmare Continues for Howard Beach Victim," the *New York Times*, January 20, 1989, p. B1.
4. Andy Logan, "Around City Hall," the *New Yorker*, January 25, 1988, pp. 101-108.
5. *Newsday*, January 4, 1987; July 7, 1987; October 14, 1987, December 23, 1987.
6. Les Payne, "Sheer Hatred Breeds Brutality," *Newsday*, January 11, 1987, p. 7.
7. *Village Voice*, February 16, 1988, p. 24, 28.

Chapter 4: JOSEPH CHRISTOPHER: MASS MURDERER

December 24-28, 1980; April 26-30, 1981; May 1-3, 7-9, 12-16, 27, 30, 1981; June 3, 30, 1981; July 12, 21, 1981; August 29, 1981; October 4, 21, 27, 1981; December 17, 1981; February 11, 1982; March 22, 24, 1982; April 13, 22, 25, 28, 1982; May 25, 1982; December 28, 1983; July 6, 1985; October 24, 1985; November 16, 1985; January 21, 1987; October 28, 1987.

Chapter 5: WILLIE TURKS: GRAVESEND

June 23-29, 1982; January 17, 1983; March 2-10, 1983; April 1, 1983; July 10, 15-16, 1983; August 5, 1983; September 3, 1983; March 15, 1984; June 13, 1984; April 16, 1985.

Chapter 6: MICHAEL STEWART: ARTIST AND MODEL

September 29-30, 1983; October 15, 20, 1983; November 2-3, 1983; January 14, 27, 1984; June 2, 9, 20, 1984; August 23, 24-25, 1984; September 15, 1984; October 6, 10, 11, 16,

1984; January 28-29, 1985; February 22-23, 1985; May 15, 1985; June 11, 18, 24, 1985; July 18, 19, 23-26, 30, 1985; August 1, 7-9, 13, 15-16, 22, 29, 1985; September 4, 7, 11, 13, 19, 21, 27, 1985; October 4-5, 8-10, 12, 17, 24, 29, 31, 1985; November 13, 25, 1985; January 4, 24, 1986; July 1, 1986; January 24-25, 31, 1987; February 10, 16, 1987; March 13, 28, 1987; October 28, 1987; January 29, 1988.

Chapter 7: ELEANOR BUMPERS: GRANDMOTHER

October 30, 1984; November 1-4, 10, 16, 18, 21-23, 27, 30, 1984; December 3, 13, 16, 21, 1984; February 1, 3, 6, 8-9, 11, 1985; April 13, 1985; April 2, 1986; November 26-27, 1986; January 13-14, 21, 28, 1987; February 3, 6, 10, 12, 18, 27-28, 1987.

Chapter 8: BERNHARD GOETZ: SUBWAY VIGILANTE

December 23-31, 1984; January 1-31, 1985; February 2-28, 1985; March 1-29, 1985; April 5, 8, 1985; Mary 15, 17, 1985; June 28-29, 1985; July 10, 29-30, 1985; August 4, 6, 8, 1985; September 12, 1985; October 6, 16, 31, 1985; November 10, 24, 26-27, 1985; December 10, 16, 17, 1985; January 17-18, 1986; March 14, 23, 1987; April 29-30, 1987; May 2-3, 5, 10, 14, 18, 20-22, 24, 26, 31, 1987; June 7, 11-13, 15, 17-18, 20-21-22, 1987; October 14, 20, 1987; November 22, 1987; March 3, 30, 1988; April 25, 1988; June 29, 1988; August 5, 1988; October 18, 1988; November 23, 1988; January 5, 14, 1989; March 4, 1989; April 29, 1989; September 20, 1989; December 2, 1989; January 10, 1990; September 27, 1990.

Chapter 9: YUSUF HAWKINS: BENSONHURST

May 29, 1986; July 3, 1986; December 27, 1987; March 13, 1988; August 25-31, 1989; September 1-4, 1989; October 2, 16, 1989; January 25, 1990; April 20, 1990; May 18-21,

24, 1990; June 12, 1990; July 4, 1990; October 2, 1990; January 12-13, 1991.

Additional information in Chapter 9 from the following:

1. Mark Bauman and Samme Chittum, "Married to the Mob: Wiseguys and Wannabes," The *Village Voice*, September 5, 1989.
2. Playthell Benjamin, "The Continuing American Tragedy: Notes on the Bensonhurst Incident," *Emerge*, November 1989, pp. 30-55.
3. Ira Glasser, "Talking Liberties: How Long, America?" *Civil Liberties* (American Civil Liberties Union), Summer 1989, p. 12.
4. Alan Weisman, "Flatbush, 60's; Bensonhurst, '89," *The New York Times*, September 5, 1989, p. A19.

Chapter 10: THE VIOLENCE CONTINUES

December 20, 1984; January 24-25, 1986; June 12, 1986; January 18, 1987; March 5, 1987; June 22, 1987; September 4-5, 1987; November 25-26, 28, 1987; December 16, 18, 24, 27, 29, 1987; March 13, 1988; May 21, 1988; October 12-13, 17, 1988; November 24, 1988; May 23-24, 27, 1989; August 5-6, 8, 1989; September 10, 12, 16, 1989; December 29, 1989; January 29, 1990; February 1, 4, 1990; March 21, 31, 1990; November 5-6, 1990; December 23, 1990; March 21, 1991.

Chapter 11: THE END

1. The *New York Times*, March 8, 1987.
2. *Ibid.*, December 30, 1987.
3. *Ibid.*, December 29, 1986.
4. *Ibid.*, August 30, 1989.
5. *Ibid*, September 6, 1989.
6. Gilbert Osofsky, *Harlem: The Making of a Ghetto*, New York: Harper and Row, 1963, p. 45.
7. *Ibid.*

8. *Ibid.*
9. The *New York Age*, January 26, 1905.
10. Osofsky, *op. cit.*, p. 81.
11. *Ibid.*, pp. 82-83.
12. Alan Weisman, "Flatbush, 60's; Bensonhurst, '98," the *New York Times*, September 5, 1989, p. A19.
13. Jim Brown (with Steve Delsohn), *Out of Bounds*, New York: Zebra Books, 1989, p. 66.

INDEX

INDEX